Adventures in Action Research

Matthew B. Courtney, Ed.D.

Adventures in Action Research

Matthew B. Courtney, Ed.D.

LEONARDWOOD
··· EDUCATIONAL PRESS ···

ISBN: 979-8-9856898-2-2

Acknowledgements

This book would not have been possible without the support of my team of practitioners and peer reviewers: Carrie Rogers, Jason Reeves, Kelly Foster, Morgan Lovitt, and Sarah Peace.

Quick Reference Guide

This book is not meant to be read from cover to cover. A list of topics is presented here to help you quickly find each section when you need to reference them later. If this is your first time through the book, please start on page 11.

From the Author

Greetings! I'm Matthew Courtney, and I help schools help kids. I am so excited to be going on this continuous improvement adventure with you! I first learned the value of action research during my second year of teaching. I taught elementary general music, which meant that over the course of a day, I would see roughly two hundred kids, in groups of twenty-five to thirty, in thirty-minute increments with no time in between. You can imagine the variety of struggles that this type of classroom schedule can create. I would like to say I handled them all deftly, but we both know that's a lie. So let's focus on one problem I did solve.

In my classroom, my number one nemesis was the unsharpened pencil. Teaching two hundred students back to back with limited time in between meant that I ended every day with about eighty broken pencils. If I was lucky, I could trick a teacher's kid into sitting in my room after school sharpening them until the sharpener eventually overheated and shut down for the day. If I was unlucky, I would run out of fresh pencils before lunch, costing me countless hours of instructional time as students waited in line for my sharpener to give their pencil new life.

This issue seems trivial now, but looking back, the matter of unsharpened pencils was a persistent problem of practice that was dramatically impacting my classroom environment. It created constant classroom management problems and took up valuable time that I could have used planning instruction, providing individualized feedback to my students, or having dinner with my family.

Unknowingly at the time, I turned to action research to solve my problem. One day after school, I was doing some required reading for a professional learning session about a writers' workshop when I stumbled upon a side note about the benefits of allowing students to write with a pen. As a music teacher, writing with pens is a big no-no. I didn't even carry pens when I was in college, because you never, ever, never-ever, ever-ever write on a piece of music with an ink pen. But I was desperate for a solution to my pencil problem, so I kept reading.

Teaching students to write measures of music isn't that different from teaching them to write pages of prose. If the dreaded ink pen could offer benefits to students in English class, maybe it could benefit them in my music classroom too. I found some research literature about other benefits to using pens, some documented techniques for teaching students to edit with ink, and some thoughtful readings on student development and functional pen use. That weekend, I went to the office supply store and bought one hundred brand-new ballpoint pens.

The next week, as my kids filed into the classroom, they each took a pen from the basket and a sheet of music paper from the tray as they found their seats. I started my lesson as usual, and to my delight, not a single student was up roaming around the room. There was no line at the pencil sharpener. I found myself teaching over enthusiastic whispers instead of soul-killing pencil grinding. It was a wonderful moment, but in my mind, just a fluke. *It was the novelty of the pens that solved the problem today*, I thought, *but it won't be a long-term solution.*

I placed a mark on the calendar, and during each class session for two weeks, I kept tallies on a variety of behaviors. I tallied any time a student got out of their seat. I tallied any time a student had an issue with their pen. I tallied any time a student filled their music paper and needed a second sheet. To my surprise, the behaviors continued to improve! I started tracking other things—like how many measures of music my students could write in a half hour. That increased too! Since they couldn't erase, I taught them special editing symbols. This helped me learn more about the types of mistakes they were making and self-correcting. After a month of data collection, I placed my tired, old pencil sharpener in the closet and never looked back.

It would be a few more years before I realized that this desperate attempt to solve my pencil problem was, in fact, action research. As my career progressed, I continued to turn to research to help me solve problems. When I transitioned out of the classroom to work on school improvement efforts, action research became one of the most powerful tools in my toolbelt. Its focused, timely, and momentum-creating methods have helped me empower countless educators to innovate, solve their own problems, and improve teaching and learning conditions for themselves and their students.

In this book, I will take you step by step through the action research process from beginning to end. We will review literature, create innovative solutions, and run casual, in-the-moment experiments to help us understand the impact of our ideas. It's okay to feel a little apprehensive—the best adventures begin from a place of uncertainty. You aren't in this alone. This book is supported by online videos and digital tools to ensure your success, and I will be with you every step of the way.

How to Use This Book

This isn't an ordinary action research manual. This book has been carefully designed to help you navigate the toughest problems of practice with ease. You will begin with a brief introduction to the action research process. In this section, I will provide an overview of the steps in the process to help you find your way. Think of this section like a roadmap; its purpose is to give you the big picture so that you will always know where you are, where you've been, and where you're going next.

At the end of each section, you have a choice to make. Will you run for the hills, or will your adventure continue? This book isn't meant to be read from cover to cover. The choices you make along the way will help guide you toward a finished product that you can be proud of. Each section ends with a list of choices that will take you on to the next step of a research project that is custom tailored to your needs. Each time you turn to this book to help you solve a problem, your path will be different.

Your first time through the book, I suggest you work through a project from start to finish, allowing each section to send you to the appropriate next step and page number. This will guarantee your success as you work to solve a persistent problem of practice. In later readings, you may decide to start at a certain point in the journey that allows you to build off work you have previously done. This is why I have placed a table of contents at the beginning of the book; it's a reference for you to use later as opposed to a series of essays to be followed in order.

What This Book Is Not

This book is not a heavy, theoretical tome. It is a book for practicing educators seeking to solve the day-to-day problems that are driving them mad. It is a book designed to help you work smarter not harder by empowering you to design and test interventions in real time.

As such, it is not a book that is going to teach you deep research theories. There will be no discussions on important research concepts (like epistemology) and only limited discussion on the study design elements necessary to complete action research projects. Some important study design elements that have whole books dedicated to them may only receive a half-page description in this book. That is all by design. The goal of this book is to get you up and running with new action research skills as quickly as possible. I've written it with the knowledge that, once you're hooked, you will dig deeper into research theory and other necessary skills later and only when you're ready for them.

Supporting Materials

Since it can be hard to learn new skills from books alone, I have created several supplemental and supporting materials that go along with this book. You can access these resources by visiting https://www.matthewbcourtney.com/actionresearch. On this page, you will find video tutorials, practice exercises, and analysis tools to help you dig deeper into the skills taught in this book.

You also have access to a section of my website called The Repository (https://www.matthewbcourtney.com/repository). The Repository is a free space where educators can learn more about data analysis and research skills. There you will find auto-analysis tools that will help you apply advanced statistical techniques with just a few clicks and videos that demonstrate new spreadsheet skills and outline helpful research workflows, as well as downloadable resources and opportunities to sign up for live webinars. The Repository is a living space and is updated regularly based on user feedback. I hope you will check it out and let me know how I can make it an even more user-friendly space for educators like you.

One last thing…

Before you dive into the sections that follow, I want to provide a word of advice. New adventures can be scary, and for many of us, the idea of producing a research project can be downright terrifying! We have horrid memories of research classes gone awry. Memories of college processors more concerned with the placement of a comma than the content of a paragraph. It's okay–I've been there too. Research isn't supposed to be a miserable moment that you must simply endure; it's supposed to be fun!

I have taught many educators to use action research to solve problems in their schools and classrooms. I can say with some certainty that you will experience moments of great frustration before you experience moments of great clarity. That is normal. I can say with some certainty that you will feel a wide range of emotions from elation to frustration, from curiosity to bewilderment. That is normal. I can say with some certainty that you will have days where your progress is rapid and days that you want to put this book on the shelf and quit. That is normal too.

Over the years, I have developed a personal motto that I encourage all my students, mentees, and readers to adopt:

Embrace the productive disequilibrium.

Do you know how sometimes when you're learning something new, everything can feel off-kilter? Do you ever have to read a paragraph four times in a row because it just won't sink in? Are you ever overcome with imposter syndrome and worry that you have drifted way off base? In those moments, you have a choice. You can give in to the fear, discomfort, and frustration of the learning process and stop, or you can embrace that moment and push through to find a level of progress and productivity. That is embracing the productive disequilibrium.

By allowing ourselves to feel vulnerable and uncomfortable and focusing on the progress that we have made, we can push through difficult learning experiences. I promise that if you embrace the productive disequilibrium, you will come out on the other side of this book a better researcher and a better-informed educator.

By purchasing this book, you have become a part of my personal network. I want you to consider me a friend and resource. Reach out to me through my website (https://www.matthewbcourtney.com/) when you get stuck and need a pep talk. I will be there to help you through a tough learning moment or to unpack a concept that isn't quite sinking in. Know that you aren't alone in this process.

Are you ready to start your adventure? Your first choice is below. Good luck on your journey, friend! May it be fruitful and gratifying.

CHOOSE YOUR PATH

If you're already ready to quit, take some time to reflect on the emotions you are feeling and choose to embrace the productive disequilibrium! Then turn to page 17 for a brief introduction to the theory behind action research.

If you're feeling excited and are ready to get started on your own path to school improvement, turn to page 17 for a brief introduction to the theory behind action research.

A Brief Introduction to Action Research

Action research is a practitioner-focused method of problem-solving that allows educators to apply the scientific method to real-world problems as they seek real-world solutions. It is an ideal protocol for practitioners in the field who are struggling with hard questions and persistent problems that they can't seem to overcome. It is also a valuable continuous improvement tool designed to delve deeply into a problem of practice and methodically test and analyze a proposed solution.

Action research is rooted in the continuous improvement work performed by Kurt Lewin in the 1940s and was popularized in education by Richard Sagor in the early 2000s with his book *Guiding School Improvement with Action Research*. It is about deep understanding through rigorous evaluation. Let's begin our adventure together by taking a broad look at the various components of a successful action research project. Think of this section like a quick primer—we will dive deeply into each of the elements later on.

The Action Research Process

Action research provides a stable, predictable, and replicable process for practitioners to follow as they seek to answer persistent problems of practice. This process mirrors the traditional scientific method deployed by research scientists in a variety of fields. The figure on the next page depicts the action research process.

The action research process begins by asking a question. A good research question should be situated around an existing problem of practice—a problem that you just can't seem to wrap your head around. Having asked a question, you then turn to the existing research literature to gain a deeper understanding of the current thinking around your problem. During this stage, you will discover how prior researchers have sought to solve your problem, identify gaps in the literature that your research could fill, and learn new theories that you could apply to your problem. All this new learning is used to form your research hypothesis—or the potential solution to your problem that you want to study. Finally, you will design an experiment, analyze the results, and uncover new insights that can inform your work.

The Action Research Process

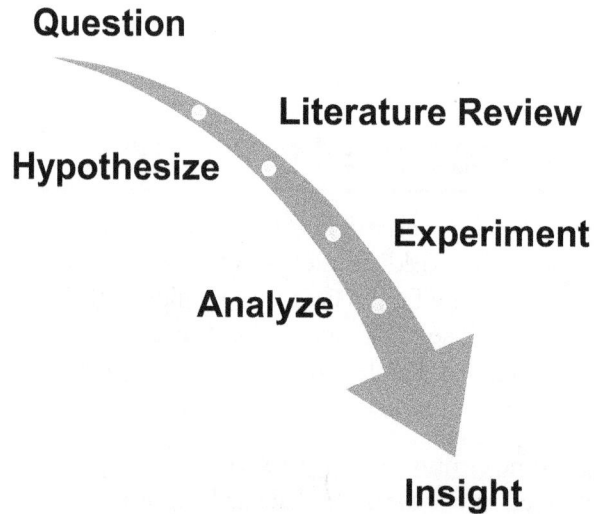

Question

Literature Review

Hypothesize

Experiment

Analyze

Insight

Identifying a Problem of Practice and Writing a Research Question

Quality action research projects respond to persistent problems of practice. These are usually deep-seated issues that are consistently causing a negative impact on teaching and learning. Before you can begin your action research project, you must undergo a period of self-reflection and observation. Consider the things that are working well for you and determine areas in which you are consistently underperforming.

Once you have identified a problem of practice, you must transform that into a research question that can be studied. It is unlikely that a truly persistent problem of practice has only a single root cause to be reviewed and resolved. It is much more likely that you will begin to see many underlying issues as you tease out your problem and begin to think about possible solutions.

Your action research project must seek to answer a question. Later in this book, you will learn how to transform your observations and problems into effective research questions. Don't stress too much about your question at the very beginning. It will evolve and develop greater clarity as you progress through the process.

Examining Existing Research Literature

The next phase in the action research process is to examine your question and gain a deeper understanding of it by reviewing the existing research literature. The goal here is to allow the existing body of knowledge on your topic to help you understand the history, points of view, and past efforts related to your question.

Through this process, you will identify keywords related to your research question, search those terms in a research database, and download and read articles that will help you learn more about your question. This book will provide a replicable and systemic approach to performing a literature review using a cyclical technique that is designed to help you quickly and thoroughly review the literature.

It is common for practitioner researchers to want to skip or rush through this step in the process. Don't do that. If you hold yourself accountable to completing the steps with fidelity, you will be guaranteed a successful and information-rich project when you are done.

Designing, Implementing, and Analyzing a Study

After you have formed a clear question and have tapped into the research literature to understand the context that surrounds it, you must design and implement an experiment to try to answer your question. There are many study designs to choose from, and any of them can be deployed under the umbrella of action research. Usually, practitioner researchers rely on one of the five most common research frameworks: the randomized controlled trial, the quasi-experimental study, the correlational study, single-case study, and qualitative study.

Randomized controlled trials, or RCTs, are experiments in which the researcher divides the study participants into two distinct groups. The first group, the control group, goes about life as normal. The second group, the intervention group, receives an intervention. At the end of the study, the researcher deploys inferential statistical methods to compare the performance of the two groups and measures the impact of the intervention.

RCTs are often considered to be the gold standard in research design. The randomization of participants helps to filter out confounding factors—or elements that may influence the outcome of the study. This type of study design lends itself to the examination of educational interventions, teaching strategies, or the deployment of programs because it allows you to clearly and accurately compare the performance of two groups. It can be challenging to perform a rigorous RCT in education because they are often very expensive, can take a long time, and are difficult to monitor as the population of a school or classroom is ever changing.

Quasi-experimental designs are similar to RCTs in that they compare the performance of two groups—a control group and an intervention group. The difference here is that the groups are previously assigned groups, such as schools or classrooms. For example, a researcher may deploy an intervention in Mr. Campbell's and Ms. Stein's fifth grade classes but not in Ms. Foster's or Mr. Napier's classes. At the end of the study, inferential statistics are deployed to measure the impact of the intervention.

Quasi-experimental studies are common in education because researchers have quick and ready access to previously assigned groups of students. However, this type of study is less rigorous than an RCT due to the prevalence of confounding factors. A lot goes into why Johnny is assigned to Mr. Napier's or Ms. Stein's classroom. Students are rarely randomly assigned to their teacher. So by using these previously assigned groups to study an intervention, the researcher is unable to account for the fact that Mr. Napier's class has all of the students with individual education plans because he is dual certified to teach both fifth grade and special education.

Some types of activities cannot be studied effectively using RCT or quasi-experimental groups. In those instances, correlational study designs may be appropriate. A correlational study design is when we look to determine if a relationship exists between an activity and an outcome. This relationship, called a correlation, can tell us the strength of a relationship but cannot tell us if one thing caused another thing. This makes correlational studies less rigorous when trying to determine the effectiveness of an intervention.

Correlational studies are handy for studies that include surveys or archival data. Any time the researcher needs to make an inference about a population, a correlational study can provide a useful framework. Correlational studies are also useful in the planning stages of larger, longitudinal studies that use an RCT or quasi-experimental design. If a correlation does not exist, it is very likely that an RCT or quasi-experimental study will find a similar result. By completing a cheaper, faster correlational study, a researcher can save time and money for more rigorous studies later.

Single-case designs are commonly deployed in schools in the special education setting. In a single-case study design, the researcher documents a phenomenon as it relates to a single observation (a student in most cases). Single-case designs usually deploy an ABA methodology, in which a baseline set of data is collected (A), then an intervention is deployed and more data are collected (B), then the intervention is removed, and a third set of data are collected (A). These phases are sometimes called baseline, intervention, and reversal phases.

This type of study helps the researcher to understand how an intervention impacts the outcomes on a single pupil. The analysis can help measure the impact of an intervention and determine if the intervention has a long-term or short-term impact. When multiple single-case studies are performed using the same intervention, they begin to form a body of research that can help future educators choose effective interventions for their individual students.

Finally, qualitative studies are those that seek to understand a phenomenon through the use of document or interview analysis. These types of studies work great if you want to study the impact of a policy decision or understand how historical barriers have impacted a population of students in your school.

Most action research projects are going to deploy either the quasi-experimental design or the single-case design depending on the scope of the problem at hand. Regardless of which method you choose, you want to make sure you build a robust and reliable data collection system that allows you to monitor the progress of your experiment and determine the impacts of your intervention. As you progress through this book, you will be asked to make choices that will lead you down the correct path.

Sharing the Results and Making a Decision

The final piece of the action research process is to share your results and make a decision. Your efforts are meaningless if nobody ever sees them or if you ignore the results. You must take steps to transparently share your work with your team and allow the findings of your action research to inform your decisions.

Start by sharing your work with your team. Your professional learning communities (PLC), faculty meetings, or other collaborative settings provide a safe space to share your work and think through its meaning. As a practitioner researcher, you likely designed your project to examine a hyper-localized problem of practice. By bringing these local teams together to hear about your work, you can learn from their collective expertise and design a local solution to your problem of practice.

To facilitate these meetings, create a slide deck that highlights each step of the process. Start by featuring your original observation and explaining how it led to the research question you posed. Discuss the key takeaways from the literature you reviewed and how that literature informed the design of your experiment. Take your audience through each phase of your experiment and explain how you collected and analyzed the data. Then share your results and discuss what you think the findings mean for your classroom or your school. Allow the audience to engage in a free-flowing conversation about your work, and allow their collective experience and expertise to inform the next steps.

If your action research procedures were appropriately rigorous, it may be appropriate for you to share the results of your study more broadly. Research conferences and journals provide an important venue for sharing the results of action research. Studies presented in this format undergo a rigorous review before being shared, archived, and indexed to allow the study to be found by other practitioner researchers like you. It is an important step toward professionalizing the profession and elevating teaching as a science that can be mastered.

Usually, the biggest barrier to successful publication or conference presentations is your own self-doubt. Have confidence in the quality work that you have created. The publication process is frequently a long and arduous one, but your persistence will pay off in the long run when future educators are using your classroom experience to inform their teaching practice.

Ethical Considerations

When conducting action research projects, there are a few important ethical considerations that we must review. While the methodologies included within the action research umbrella are unlikely to cause harm to individuals, practitioner researchers should work to maintain the highest level of ethical professionalism throughout their work.

Institutes of higher education and educator licensing boards usually have codes of ethics that guide and govern professional behavior. If you are working under one of those two paradigms, you should pause your reading now to locate and review the official ethics documents of your institution or licensing board. If you don't fall into one of these two categories, then I suggest reviewing the Code of Ethics published by the American Education Research Association (AERA). You can access their Code of Ethics at https://www.aera.net/about-aera/aera-rules-policies/professional-ethics.

While a review of these documents will provide you with a deep understanding of your professional ethical responsibilities, I want to dedicate some space here to hitting the highlights and exploring some of the most important ethical considerations for the action research context.

Avoiding Harm

As a practitioner researcher, your first and most important ethical responsibility is to ensure that your work does not lead to direct or indirect harm of any participant in your study. Apply a broad understanding of the word *harm* when considering this ethical responsibility. You must work to prevent physical harm, emotional harm, psychological harm, academic harm, social harm, and economic harm as you pursue your action research project. If you become aware of instances of harm caused by your study, your ethical responsibility requires you to terminate your project and to actively work to resolve any issue you may have caused.

Avoiding Discrimination and Exploitation

As a practitioner researcher, you must work to actively avoid discrimination and exploitation through your work. For our purposes here, discrimination means that you have made a concerted effort to avoid unjust or prejudicial treatment of individuals due to their identity. Each state has its own list of identities for which it is considered illegal to discriminate, but practitioner researchers should carefully monitor for discrimination among all forms of identity. Common identity characteristics to consider include race, ethnicity, nationality, culture, gender expression and gender identity, sex, sexual orientation, age, religion, ability or disability, health conditions, socioeconomic status, marital status, or parental status.

Another ethical consideration related to discrimination is exploitation. Exploitation is when a practitioner researcher leverages a position of power to treat someone unfairly to derive a personal or professional benefit. Exploitation may look like active manipulation, intentionally sharing misinformation or withholding information from a subordinate, or coercive threats designed to change a behavior. Practitioner researchers must actively work to avoid exploitation of those in their care.

Maintaining Confidentiality

Many times, practitioner researchers will find themselves working with confidential information. They have an ethical responsibility to ensure that confidential information remains confidential. This information may include data sets, interview transcripts, or other observation materials. Practitioner researchers should proactively work to establish methods for collecting and storing data that ensures confidentiality is maintained.

The practitioner researcher must also remain aware of the confidentiality requirements of their positions and licensing boards. At times, it may be appropriate for a practitioner researcher to break confidentiality to protect the life and safety of a student. In those instances, practitioner researchers should refer to their local policy and procedure documents.

Ensuring Informed Consent

Practitioner researchers must ensure that they provide informed consent any time they are working directly with a human subject. Informed consent means that the individuals involved in your action research project know that they are involved and have agreed to participate. Any time you are conducting an experiment within your school or system, you should collect informed consent documentation from your study participants or their parents.

If your work includes publicly accessible data sources, such as administrative data sets, then informed consent is not necessary.

Sharing Your Work

When your project is complete, the practitioner researcher has an ethical obligation to share their work. You should share your work openly and honestly, without omitting data elements or attempting to present your work in an inaccurate manner. Be as transparent as possible—even if your experiment didn't work. That is valuable information that your fellow researchers need to know. As always, make sure that you are sharing your work within the regulations of your own professional setting and licensing requirements.

Research Biases

When conducting action research, practitioner researchers must be aware of the various types of bias that may be introduced during the research process. I'm not talking here about bias that may impact instruction or access such as implicit bias, racial bias, or gender bias. I am talking about research biases that may impact the types of data included in the analysis or the procedures applied. While some degree of bias is unavoidable—no analyst or researcher can ever be perfect—practitioner researchers must be on the lookout for cases of extreme bias and be prepared to consider the impact of that bias on their processes.

Let's begin our discussion by looking at sampling and selection bias. These two biases are related to how we select the study participants. Sampling bias occurs when a study sample includes only a specific type of participant (inclusion bias) or doesn't include an impacted population (omission bias), when it only includes participants who have been identified as needing a specific intervention (channeling bias), or when it includes a group of individuals already assembled and available to the researcher (convenience bias).

When you set out to begin your action research project, sampling and selection biases are the first thing to check for. You should take steps to carefully consider whether you have chosen the right study designs, populations, and data sources to answer your question or if you have unintentionally avoided certain types of data.

Consider the following example. The new chair of the English Department wants to know if the curriculum adopted three years ago is having a positive impact on students. When he accesses the database to select the relevant administrative and assessment data for his analysis, he must ensure that he is pulling appropriate and complete data. Let's say that the new chair doesn't like the curriculum. This may lead him to unconsciously introduce inclusion bias into his sample by only accessing data points for students in general or remedial sections while leaving out students enrolled in the advanced level courses, despite the knowledge that all three levels deploy the same foundational curriculum. By leaving out the data for the advanced students, the new department chair is likely to achieve a result that skews low, which is what he subconsciously wanted to see.

Sampling and selection bias aren't inherently bad. Sometimes they are necessary. If you are studying the impact of a behavior intervention on one single student, you are engaging in channeling bias. You are performing a study on a student who was selected due to their previously established need to undergo an intervention. That can be an appropriate procedure. Your job as a practitioner researcher is to consider whether bias has been introduced into a sample and how that bias may have impacted the results of the analysis.

Another type of bias that impacts practitioner researchers is response bias. Response bias represents another category of bias that is common in study designs that rely on interviews, observations, or survey instruments. Response bias is introduced when the respondent changes their answers or behaviors due to action taken by the researcher. Two common forms of response bias are acquiescence bias and social desirability bias.

Acquiescence bias is when a respondent gives an answer they think the researcher is looking for. If it is very clear that the researcher is hoping for one outcome over another, respondents may unintentionally change their answer to a question in an unconscious act of empathy–hoping to help the researcher achieve their desired goals. This is common when educators seek feedback directly from student or parent groups with whom they have strong relationships and bonds. These groups want to see the teachers and schools be successful and may not always give their honest opinions when completing surveys or interviews.

Social desirability bias is similar in that a respondent may provide an answer that they think is preferable based on societal norms, even if that answer doesn't reflect their true feelings on a situation. Social desirability bias is common in settings where groups of participants are interviewed together. A respondent with a contrary point of view may be less willing to voice that opinion due to the unconscious social pressures created by the group. Similarly, activities such as student or teacher observation are prone to social desirability bias. If a teacher knows that their administrator is counting the number of higher order questions asked in a specific thirty-minute period, they are likely to unconsciously boost the number of higher order questions during their observation period in an effort to respond to the social pressures.

Interviewer or observer bias is similar in that respondents may change their answers in an attempt to please the interviewer or observer. The difference here is that the change in response comes as a reaction to a behavior performed by the researcher. Simple things like vocal inflection or facial expressions can influence the behaviors and answers of the respondents. When collecting feedback data through interviews and surveys, it is important that educators maintain a neutral demeanor to avoid influencing the outcome.

Finally, results bias occurs when a practitioner researcher changes, suppresses, or spins the results of their analysis in a desirable manner. One of the most common forms of results bias is confirmation bias. Confirmation bias is when the researcher spins the results to tell the narrative that they want to tell. Another common form of results bias is publication bias. Publication bias occurs when a researcher, decision-maker, or publisher chooses not to publish negative results from an analysis. This is sometimes colloquially called "file folder bias" because the researcher just leaves their results in a file folder, never to be heard from again.

Results bias is problematic when using research to drive continuous improvement because if you are changing or hiding negative results, your decisions will be inherently misinformed. Practitioner researchers must make sure that they are always sharing the truth of the data, even when the truth hurts.

It is impossible for a practitioner researcher to avoid all types of bias. Bias is inherent in our lives and is almost always unintentional, but with careful attention, it can be mostly avoided. One way to avoid bias in your action research project is to work as part of a team. Ensure that each member of your team is committed to honest and transparent research processes and cultivate a culture where each member of the team feels comfortable questioning decisions along the way. If one member of the team suggests leaving out a data point or downplaying a finding, it is the responsibility of the other members to probe that decision and come to a consensus.

Another great way to avoid bias is to establish protocols and norms for your project. Take time to consider how biases may influence your protocol and eliminate them from the start. You should also review your protocols periodically to make sure that no new biases have slipped into your process or were missed when they were developed.

In my opinion, one of the best ways to avoid bias is through transparency. As they say, sunlight is the best disinfectant. By openly and transparently sharing your process and the results of your analysis with your colleagues and other relevant stakeholders, they can help you find things that you may have missed. Be humble and open to questioning when you present your work and commit to hearing all criticisms through a lens of curiosity.

Conclusion

As you work through this book, you will engage deeply in the action research process. You will develop questions, review literature, design a study, analyze the results, and report on your findings. This task may feel daunting, but never fear–the materials presented here will walk you through the process step by step.

Remember that the purpose of action research is to help the actor improve their actions, so let your personality and professional experience guide your work. Action research projects should be fun! Don't think about this the same way you viewed homework assignments in grad school. You are a problem-solver seeking to better understand what's going on in your classroom. Allow the action research framework to be a road map on your adventure, but make the adventure your own along the way.

CHOOSE YOUR PATH

After reflecting on the action research process, turn to page 29 to begin your action research project by crafting a research question.

Crafting a Research Question

The first step in the action research process is to create a question rooted in observation. Remember that action research is meant to help practitioners resolve a persistent problem of practice. Spend some time thinking about the various issues that you face in your professional life. Perhaps you have a classroom management challenge that you aren't sure how to handle, or maybe you have a group of students who is consistently low performing. Are you implementing a new policy that you aren't sure is going to work? Try to choose a problem that is going to make a significant impact on your life if you can resolve it.

Once you have identified your problem of practice, the next step is to do a root cause analysis to try to identify the underlying causes of your problem. My favorite root cause analysis protocol is The Five Whys. Simply ask yourself why a problem exists, then why does that barrier exist? Continue asking why five times until you get down to a root cause. Here is an example:

Problem: Mr. Norton's students are always late to class.

1. Why? Because the passing period was shortened this year by the school's administration.
    2. Why? Because too many students were getting into trouble during the passing period.
        3. Why? Because they were spending too much time idle in the hallways.
            4. Why? Because they weren't motivated to get to class early.
                5. Why? Because there was nothing for them to do.

Through this procedure, we can see that the real root cause of the issue is that students don't feel motivated to get to class before the bell rings because there is nothing for them to do while they wait. This becomes the foundation of an action research project.

Next, take the root cause you have identified and transform it into a research question. A good research question is a clear and focused statement that expresses the problem you are seeking to better understand. It forecasts to the world what you are hoping to accomplish and provides a subtle glimpse into how you might get there.

Transforming an observation or a wondering into a meaningful research question is easy. Start by writing your statement out, then do a quick quality check by asking yourself these questions:

- Is it clear? Your research question should be able to stand on its own. The reader should understand what you're seeking to answer without any supporting explanation.

- Is it focused? Channel your inner Goldilocks. Your question shouldn't be too narrow nor too broad. Make sure it centers on a single issue that you can answer directly.

- Is it complex? A quality research question should be answered only through discussion. If your question can be answered with a simple yes or no, then you should return to the drawing board.

- Is it arguable? It's time to put on your ornery hat and get ready to argue! Your research question should allow you to take and defend a specific position. It should also leave room for your opposition to take and defend theirs.

- Is it relevant? When crafting your research question, take care to ensure that your question addresses the observations you made in your data. Question drift is a common cause of continuous improvement catastrophes.

Let's continue with our example. Mr. Norton now knows that his students are bored waiting for the bell to ring, so he wants to study the issue by asking the question: **Will students get to class on time if they have an assignment waiting for them?**

Can you answer "yes" to each of the five guiding questions above? Let's see…

- Is it clear? Sort of. I know that Mr. Norton wants to use an assignment to get his students to class on time, but I don't know what kind of assignment.

- Is it focused? No. The question is pretty broad and leaves a lot of room for interpretation.

- Is it complex? No. This question has a simple yes or no answer.

- Is it arguable? Not really. While you may be able to argue a yes or no response at the end, the question isn't setting Mr. Norton up for a discourse that will allow him to truly understand the impact of his new assignment policy.

- Is it relevant? Yes. The question is related to Mr. Norton's identified root cause.

We can do better. We know that we need a question that is a bit more focused and a bit more arguable. So let's try this one: **How does the incorporation of an interactive team-building activity during the passing time motivate students to get to class on time?**

How does this question stack up against our five guiding questions?

- Is it clear? Yes. I can clearly see that Mr. Norton is going to implement an interactive team-building activity during passing time and track attendance.

- Is it focused? Yes. I know exactly what Mr. Norton wants to do and hopes to accomplish.

- Is it complex? Yes. The question cannot be answered with a simple yes or no.

- Is it arguable? Yes. This question will uncover nuanced information that will allow you to take and argue a specific point of view.

- Is it relevant? Yes. The question is relevant. It is related to your observations and references a specific intervention that you hope to deploy.

This kind of research question will help lead you in the right direction. It gives you clear guidance as you start to work and helps to make sure that you will produce an outcome that will address your identified problem of practice.

As you progress through the next phases of your action research project, you should come back to periodically check in with your research question. It is likely that your research question will strengthen and evolve as you complete your literature review and design your experiment. Never fear—that's what's supposed to happen!

CHOOSE YOUR PATH

Spend some time reflecting on your professional practice. After you have chosen a problem and crafted a research question, turn to page 33 to begin the literature review process.

The Literature Review

As a researcher, your work must be rooted in a sound theoretical model. It is important that your work expands upon the current thinking in the field and allows practitioners to see how best practices have evolved over time. For your research to be taken seriously, its connection to past research must be clearly established. This process is called the literature review.

Before we consider the steps to completing a successful literature review, let us first consider the three most common types of literature review. While all literature reviews represent an author's attempt to depict the current thinking on an issue, not all literature reviews are the same. As a practitioner researcher, you must understand the difference between the common types of literature reviews so that you can make the best use of them when you come upon them as you work.

The most common type of literature review is the theoretical framework. When crafting a theoretical framework, the author pulls research from a wide variety of perspectives and constructs a narrative designed to help the reader understand the ins and outs of a specific theory. This type of literature review tends to be very focused in its scope.

While you can certainly find standalone theoretical frameworks, you will most commonly encounter them embedded within larger research papers. Researchers use theoretical frameworks to help lay the foundation for the research they have performed and to help provide context to the reader before introducing the specifics of their study. This is the type of literature review you will complete as you conduct an action research project. We will explore the individual steps for crafting a theoretical framework soon.

Like a theoretical framework, systematic reviews dig deep into the existing research literature to paint a comprehensive picture of a theory or phenomenon. This type of literature kicks up the level of rigor by following an established search methodology. The methodology section is a distinct characteristic of a systematic review that indicates to the reader that this paper has undergone a deeper process. Systematic reviews generally follow a protocol where researchers identify databases and search terms and "systematically" gather research on an issue. They then summarize the studies and synthesize them into actionable information.

Systematic reviews are incredibly valuable to education practitioners and continuous improvement specialists because they provide an in-depth analysis of the research on a very specific topic. Systematic reviews are designed to be truly comprehensive, so they give the education practitioner a good understanding of the topic. Additionally, systematic reviews are almost always published in peer reviewed journals, which makes them useful for practitioner researchers seeking a comprehensive understanding of a problem of practice.

The third type of literature review we will be discussing is the meta-analysis. A meta-analysis is a systematic review with a little math at the end. They have taken the education field by storm in the last eight to ten years, largely due to the international popularity of John Hattie's seminal work *Visible Learning* (which is really a meta-meta-analysis). In a meta-analysis, the researcher pulls research reports with statistical outcomes, then summarizes them using more statistics to attempt to create a master result.

These master results are useful for schools seeking to implement a new strategy or program. Education leaders must be able to set realistic goals and expectations for new efforts. When you read twenty articles about the results of a strategy, you get twenty different outcomes. It can be hard to synthesize that information on your own. In a meta-analysis, the researcher has done that work for you.

Creating a Theoretical Framework

As you begin your action research project, you must create a theoretical framework of your own. By taking the research question you have previously asked and diving deep into the existing research that surrounds it, you will be able to create a better project.

While you may be tempted to believe that the results of your finding are the most important part of your project, the truth is that without a properly conducted literature review, the results of your study have no meaningful impact on the field. The literature review helps the reader to understand why your research matters by first establishing a precedent for your work and then building upon it. It can be daunting to dive into the mountain of literature on your topic; therefore, the process should be approached with a carefully constructed plan. This six-step model will help set you up for success.

Search for articles.

The first step in completing a literature review is to find peer-reviewed research articles that are relevant to your study. There are many databases available to education researchers as they begin to search for prior studies on their topic. As this is an ever-changing list, I have provided direct links to some of my favorite resources on the webpage that supports this book (https://www.matthewbcourtney.com/actionresearch). You will also find video walk-throughs of each resource with specific tips and tricks for each one.

While each research database may have its own pathways, the basic steps are the same. Begin the process by coming up with a list of keywords related to your topic. Research databases are not usually as intuitive as other Internet search engines that you may be familiar with. You will want to come up with several variations of keywords surrounding your project. For example, if your project is about interventions for English learners, you may try these variations:

- English learner
- English language learner
- Bilingual students
- English acquisition

If you are planning to conduct your literature review over a period of several days or weeks, I suggest you keep a log to help you track keywords. I keep my logs in a spreadsheet and usually capture the date, the database used, the keywords deployed, and how many articles I found.

Model Spreadsheet for Tracking Keywords

	A	B	C	D
	Date	**Database**	**Keyword**	**Articles**
1	1/15/22	ERIC	English Learners	15
2	1/16/22	ERIC	Bilingual Students	21
3	1/19/22	Elicit	English Learners	11

It is likely that your initial search will yield far too many results for you to process. This is where filters come into play. All research databases will include a variety of filters to help you narrow down your search results. Consider applying some of these common filters:

- **Peer Reviewed:** A Peer Reviewed filter will sort your results and only show you those that have been published by peer reviewed research journals. These sources are considered to be of higher quality and to be more reliable than other types of publications.

- **Date Range:** If you have more results than you can handle, consider limiting the results by date range. It is common practice to start your results with a five- or ten-year range. I always like to add a one-year range too so that I can make sure I am capturing all of the most recent research on a topic.

- **Location:** Location filters will narrow your search down to only studies conducted in certain locations, such as the United States. While it can be helpful to view research conducted in your own country, don't count out research performed in other spaces. We can learn a lot from our colleagues all around the world.

2	**Read abstracts and download articles.**

Having narrowed the number of articles in your search, it is time to select the articles you want to read and use in your paper. Research databases makes this easy by providing detailed abstracts right in the search results. An abstract is a short summary of a research paper–kind of like the description on the back of a book. They help researchers choose which articles warrant a deeper read as they work on their projects.

Simply start at the top of your search results and work your way through the abstracts. You should be able to tell within the first few sentences if an article is going to meet your needs. If your database only displays the first few lines of an abstract, you can usually access a full abstract by clicking on the article title.

Once you have found an article that you want to read, download it and save it to your desktop. Don't spend time reading the articles yet. That will slow you down and cause you to circle back over your search results multiple times. Focus on building your own library of articles relevant to your topic.

Most research databases will download articles using a generic name. It is unlikely that you will be able to tell which article is which based on those generic names, so you will want to re-name each article and save it in a unique folder on your hard drive. A good way to do this is to create a master folder for your project followed by a folder with the date of your search. Give your file a recognizable name, such as the author's last name and the year it was published. This will make it easier to find files later. Keep working with this step until you have a good-sized library, twenty articles or so, that focus on your specific topic.

3	Read the articles and take notes.

Once you have collected your articles, it is time to read them and take notes. It is vitally important that you read all the articles to develop a deep understanding of the current thinking on your topic. During this process, you will want to take detailed notes in an efficient way. There are two notetaking methods that work well here.

The first method is to type all your notes into a word processing document. Start by writing the full citation for the article (this will come in handy later when you build your references list), then place your notes under the citation with bullets. Keep all the notes for all articles in the same document.

Another technique is to type your notes into a spreadsheet. For this technique, you will want to set your spreadsheet up with three columns: Author Last Name, Year of Publication, and Note. Place each note in its own row. This will allow you to sort and code the notes efficiently later.

<u>Model Spreadsheet for Notetaking</u>

	A	B	C
1	**Author**	**Year**	**Notes**
2	Name	2021	This is my note.
3	Name	2021	This is my note.
4	Name	2021	This is my note.

As you work through your articles, do not copy and paste language from the article into your notes; always paraphrase. This step helps to prevent accidental acts of plagiarism later as you will eventually paraphrase the language again when you place it into your paper.

4	**Identify new articles from your reading and find them.**

Step four isn't really a new step; it is really a subpart of step three. As you read, make notes of other articles that you need to find and read. It is likely that past authors will cite foundational articles on your topic or seminal pieces of research that you need to familiarize yourself with. You should also scan the references list of each article for article titles that sound meaningful or relevant to your paper. Keep a running list of articles as you read and find them in Step Five.

5	**Rinse and repeat.**

It is unlikely that your initial library of twenty articles has provided enough information for you to fully develop a theoretical foundation for your work. You will have to repeat the search process multiple times to develop a thorough and comprehensive review. You should repeat these steps by finding the articles you identified in Step Four and returning to Step One to test out new keywords. There is no steadfast rule as to when you have enough information. A good rule of thumb is that you have enough information when a scan of multiple reference lists turns up no new articles of interest or all the research you are reading starts to cite one another.

6	**Code your notes and craft a framework.**

Once you have completed the literature search process and taken detailed notes about your articles, the final step in the literature review process is to code your notes to identify themes. As you have read, you have undoubtedly noted themes or trends that run across the articles. Make a list of the themes then turn to your notes and identify which notes support each theme. If you used the document method, highlight each theme in a different color. If you used the spreadsheet method, you could add a column to your spreadsheet and type the codes into that column. Make sure that every note you have is aligned to a theme; you may need to add or change themes as you dig into your notes and begin to read them with this new lens. These themes will eventually become the subheadings in your literature review and will help you to present an organized and logical theoretical framework to your readers.

Transforming Literature into Theory

Having completed a thorough literature review, you must now craft a theoretical model to support your research questions and give context to your findings. If you have taken the time to complete a thorough and thoughtful literature review, then this part will be much easier. Your task is to weave the existing literature into a compelling story that tells the reader everything that they need to know to understand why your study is important. Remember, nobody is an expert at everything. You must provide sufficient background so that readers can fully understand the relevant historical and theoretical context for your study and its findings.

Here are some dos and don'ts to keep in mind as you organize your thoughts:

- **DO** use headings to group the literature by themes. Headings make it easy for the reader to quickly navigate your paper. It also makes the information easier to digest by breaking it down into topical snippets that can be stand alone.
    - **DON'T** use a heading if you don't need one. If you find that a section of your paper only includes one or two sources, it probably isn't robust enough to warrant a stand-alone section. Do some more digging for other literature or allow this section to be absorbed by another theme.

- **DO** consider the flow of the paper. You should work to make connections between themes and help the reader see how everything fits together into a big picture. Your theory model should tell a story.
    - **DON'T** be afraid to vary slightly from established academic norms. While there are time-tested formulas for presenting research papers, the best researchers know when to follow the rules and when to adjust them appropriately to make a point.

- **DO** weave multiple pieces of literature together to make your point. Think of it like baking a cake. Your literature is the cake itself–it's super important and must be put together just right in order to work, but the decoration is where you get to add a little splash of personality. Is it a wedding cake or a birthday cake? You tell me!
    - **DON'T** simply state what the prior research has said. If the reader wants to know what another researcher says about a topic, they can read the original paper.

- **DO** provide an appropriate citation every time. It is likely that you will cite a paper multiple times in your discussion of the theory—especially if it represents a new change in thinking. The paper must be cited every time you use it.
    - o **DON'T** cite studies that you didn't use. It is likely that you spent time reading papers that never actually make it into your theory model. That is okay. Don't add a study simply because you spent time on it.

- **DO** make sure to make your point. Each section of your theory should make a connection back to the purpose of your study and reiterate why your research is important. After reading each section, ask yourself, "So what?"
    - o **DON'T** give away the results of your study too soon. Your theory model is where you set up the study and help identify the glaring hole in the theory you are trying to fill. You can discuss your study later.

- **DO** allow this section to challenge the thinking of others and yourself. Your goal is to expose gaps and restructure current thinking to create space for new ideas—YOUR new ideas! You cannot do that without challenging old ways of thinking.

CHOOSE YOUR PATH

After completing your literature review and creating a compelling theoretical model, turn to page 41 to begin designing your study.

Study Design and Implementation

Once you have crafted your research question and developed a deeper understanding of your topic through the literature review process, it is time to design and implement a study. While this may sound daunting, your efforts will be supported by the existing structures and protocols already in place within the field. We call these protocols study designs. Think about a study design like a roadmap; it helps you know where you are going and what stops you will make along the way. In this section, you will learn more about the broad categories of study design. This will help you select the appropriate study design to continue along your action research journey.

Throughout your literature review process, you have undoubtedly encountered countless study design descriptions. Each researcher will include detailed descriptions of their methodology in their final reports. While you may feel a bit overwhelmed by the volume and variations of study descriptions you have reviewed, you can rest assured knowing that most studies are iterations of one of only a handful of study design categories. For our purposes, I have selected the six study designs that lend themselves most readily to the action research process.

Study designs come in two flavors: quantitative and qualitative. Quantitative study designs are those in which the researcher seeks to answer a question. In education, quantitative studies usually seek to answer questions related to the impact of educational interventions. These studies focus on rigorous data collection and analysis and almost always use statistics to help the reader understand the outcome of the study. There are five principal quantitative frameworks:

1) Randomized Controlled Trials (RCTs): An RCT is a type of experiment in which the researcher randomly sorts participants into two groups: an intervention group who receives some kind of treatment and a control group who goes about business as usual. At the end, the researcher uses descriptive and inferential statistics to determine if the treatment made a difference for the intervention group. Researchers deploy RCTs

when they want to understand the impact of an activity on a group, and they have the ability to control group assignment.

2) Quasi-Experimental Designs: A quasi-experimental study is similar to an RCT in that it compares the performance of two groups using descriptive and inferential statistics. The difference here is that the two groups are previously assigned groups, such as schools, classrooms, or districts. Researchers use quasi-experimental designs when they want to understand the impact of an activity on a group but they do not have the ability to control group assignment.

3) Single-Case Designs: Single-case designs are studies that focus on the impact of an intervention on a single student. They are sometimes called ABA designs. In a single-case study, the researcher collects baseline data (Baseline Phase or A Phase), then introduces an intervention and collects intervention period data (Intervention Phase or B Phase), then removes the intervention to see if changes in behavior were permanent (Reversal Phase or A Phase). At the end, the researcher uses descriptive and inferential statistics to see how the intervention changed the outcomes for a single student.

4) Correlational Designs: Correlational study designs are those in which a researcher wants to measure the strength of a relationship between an activity and an outcome. Correlational designs usually rely on historical or survey data and use the correlation co-efficient to measure relationships. It is important to note that correlational designs do not measure causality as the three previously mentioned designs do. You cannot say for certain that one thing caused another thing to happen—only whether the two things are related.

5) Descriptive Designs: In a descriptive study, a researcher is simply reporting on the current and historical conditions of a thing. This can be a valuable exercise for researchers seeking to understand current phenomena or those who want to see how conditions have changed over time. The steps for completing a descriptive study design are often necessary in the completion of the four previously discussed designs, making this study design the least rigorous in this list.

Qualitative studies, by contrast, are those that seek to describe and understand a phenomenon. They differ from quantitative studies in that their data usually comes from those impacted by a phenomenon and is collected through processes such as interviews, focus groups, observations, or document analysis. Instead of using statistics, qualitative researchers use a method called "coding" to sort their data into categories or themes that can be summarized and discussed.

There are a number of qualitative study designs available to researchers, including historical design, grounded theory design, phenomenology, or ethnographic design. For the purposes of action research, this book will focus on qualitative study designs from a broader perspective. It will provide only the essential steps necessary to gather information intentionally and methodically about a phenomenon to help you understand how that phenomenon has impacted a given population.

Sometimes, a researcher wants to understand an existing phenomenon but also wants to conduct an experiment or use quantitative data to help develop their understanding. These designs are called mixed-methods designs. Within the constructs of action research, a mixed-method design is one in which the researcher performs some qualitative work using the principles of phenomenology along with one of the five quantitative designs listed above. Mixed-methods designs are wonderful for inclusion in action research projects because they allow the practitioner researcher to dig deeper into the local context in which they are working.

Selecting a Study Design

As you plan to implement your action research project, it is important that you choose the right study design. There are a few key elements to consider. First, you should consider your capacity to complete the project within the given time frame. Think about your current time commitments and how your resources are spread across your work, family, and other obligations. For example, it may be unrealistic to embark on a qualitative study design that requires dozens of interviews if you are teaching full-time and have one kid in soccer and another in ballet.

You should also consider the resources available to you and your context within your school. Do you have sufficient decision-making authority to randomly sort students into control and intervention groups? If not, then you should not select the RCT study design. Consider your current access to data storehouses maintained by your district. If you do not have access to many years of historical assessment data, then a descriptive study that seeks to document changes in student performance over time is not your best bet.

Finally, consider your research question and what you really want to know at the end of your study. You want to select a research design that will allow you to answer your research question. For example, if you want to measure the impact of an intervention, then you must select from either the RCT, quasi-experimental, or single-case study designs. You will not be able to answer your question with any other study design. Similarly, if you want to understand the impact of a policy decision on your students, then you will want to select from the correlational, descriptive, or qualitative study designs. It is now time to choose the next step in your journey. Consider the options below and choose a study design that makes sense for your project.

CHOOSE YOUR PATH

Do you want to understand the impact of an intervention on two groups of randomly assigned students? Turn to page 45 to learn how to perform a randomized controlled trial.

Do you want to understand the impact of an intervention on two previously assigned groups of students? Turn to page 51 to learn how to conduct a quasi-experimental study.

Do you want to understand the impact of an intervention on a single student? Turn to page 57 to learn how to conduct a single-case study.

Do you want to understand the strength of the relationship between two variables? Turn to page 63 to learn how to conduct a correlational study.

Do you want to report on the current state of a phenomenon? Turn to page 63 to learn how to conduct a descriptive study.

Do you want to understand how people feel about and/or are impacted by a phenomenon? Turn to page 69 to learn about qualitative study design.

Do you want to use a combination of the study designs mentioned here? Begin your mixed-methods study by selecting one of the quantitative study designs above along with the qualitative study design option.

Randomized Controlled Trial

Randomized controlled trials, or RCTs, are considered to be the most rigorous category of study design. They consist of experiments in which the researcher divides the study participants into two distinct groups. The first group, the control group, goes about life as normal. The second group, the intervention group, receives an intervention. At the end of the study, the researcher uses descriptive and inferential statistics to understand the impact of the intervention.

The key word here is random. In an RCT, study participants are randomly assigned to one of the two groups, and they don't know which of the two groups they have been assigned to. The randomization of participants helps to filter out confounding factors–or elements that may influence the outcome of the study. Confounding factors are common within existing educational groups because a great deal of thought goes into how we assign students to groups. We may group students by performance level, assign them to a teacher with a special skill set or past experience, or intentionally assign two students to two different homerooms in order to avoid classroom management problems. While these intentional choices can be good for individual student outcomes, they create challenges for action research projects. Random sampling strips those confounding factors away by placing all study participants on an equal footing.

The RCT lends itself well to the examination of educational interventions, teaching strategies, or the deployment of programs because it allows you to clearly and accurately compare the performance of two groups.

To conduct an RCT in your classroom, follow these steps:

1	Identify your intervention and select your study participants.

If you haven't done so already, now is the time to determine which intervention you will be deploying to try to solve your problem of practice. You should have a good idea of which types of interventions may improve your situation based on the literature review that you conducted earlier.

Once you have selected your intervention, you will need to identify your study participants. It is important that you select study participants that are flexible enough for you to be able to control their group assignments.

2	Randomly sort your participants into two groups: an intervention and a control group.

To perform an RCT, you must sort your participants into two randomly assigned groups. For this step, you have a couple of options.

The first option is to randomly sort all participants into two groups. This is easily accomplished using spreadsheet software. To perform this task, open a fresh spreadsheet and place your full roster of study participants into Column A. In Column B, use a combination of the **CHOOSE** and **RANDBETWEEN** functions to randomly assign an "Intervention" or "Control" label as follows: **=CHOOSE(RANDBETWEEN(1,2), "Intervention", "Control")**.

Model Spreadsheet for Randomization

	A	B
1	**Participant Names**	**Category**
2	Name	Intervention
3	Name	Control
4	Name	Intervention

Another common method of randomization is called "stratified random assignment." This random assignment protocol is appropriate if you want to examine the impact of an intervention on different groups, such as typically high vs. low performing students, students with disabilities vs. students without disabilities, or students in one school vs. those in another school.

To complete this two-step process, begin by setting up a new spreadsheet with all your participants in Column A. In Column B, document your stratification groups. Within each group, apply the randomization protocol discussed above to ensure that you have participants from each stratification group in both the intervention and the control groups.

Model Spreadsheet for Stratified Random Assignment

	A	B	C
1	**Participant Names**	**Stratification Group**	**Category**
2	Name	Group A	Intervention
3	Name	Group A	Control
4	Name	Group B	Intervention

3	Identify/create your evaluation instrument(s).

Before you can begin your study, you need to identify and/or create your evaluation instruments. Your evaluation instruments are the tools you will use to gather the data necessary to determine if your intervention provided the desired outcome. Here are a few important considerations when selecting your evaluation instrument.

- Whenever possible, try to select a previously established evaluation instrument. A high quality independently developed instrument helps to ensure that the results of your study are measured accurately. These previously designed instruments could be standardized tests, published surveys, assessments included within a curriculum, standardized classroom observation instruments, or something similar.

- If you are seeking to evaluate the impact of a program or curriculum that includes evaluation instruments, try to find a different evaluation instrument that aligns with your study objectives. If you rely on the evaluation instruments housed within a packaged intervention, you may be assessing a student's ability to achieve within the program and not necessarily whether the student has achieved in an outcome aligned to the underlying learning target.

- If you plan to use a survey to measure changes in behavior or perception, the research literature may help you identify commonly used and respected surveys that already exist in the field. Before using a survey, contact the author of those surveys to ask for permission and be sure to cite their work when you present about your project.

- If you are creating your own instrument from scratch, take care to ensure that it is both valid and reliable. You could pilot your instrument on a small group of individuals who are not part of your study by administering your instrument twice with about a month in between. You can use a t-test (see page 86) to see if the two administrations were statistically similar. You should also have a team of colleagues review your instrument to see if they think it accurately assesses the intended outcome.

4	Collect some baseline data.

To understand how the performance of your participants has changed after the intervention, you must measure where they are before they begin to receive the intervention. This is called baseline data. Before you begin your study, take time to collect detailed demographic data and baseline assessment data on each participant.

Demographic data is an important component that will help you better understand the impact of the intervention on your participants in the end. This is especially important if you have students from a variety of identities or school-created labels (such as special education or low-income labels). Take time to think about all the various demographic elements you could collect on your participants and gather that information up front. It is easier to get this information from your participants at the beginning than to try to go back and collect demographic information after the study has concluded.

You should also deploy your previously selected evaluation instrument and gather some baseline data. Depending on your project, this baseline data collection may include administering your evaluation protocol in its entirety as a pre-test, or it may involve gathering previously collected data (such as behavior data, attendance data, or standardized assessment data) from an existing information system.

The last step before you begin to implement your intervention is to check for baseline equivalency. During this process, you will want to take a careful look at the data for your intervention and control groups to see how similar they are. If your group is large and you have properly performed a randomization protocol, your two groups should be similar. If your groups are not similar, you could run your randomization protocol again. If you ran a full group randomization and ended up with two very unbalanced groups, you could try switching to a stratified random assignment protocol. Whatever you do, do not manually move participants from one group to another to achieve balance. Doing so would undo your random assignment and introduce bias into your study.

5	Implement your intervention.

Having established your intervention, selected your participants, randomly sorted them into groups, and gathered some baseline data, you are now ready to perform your intervention! This is where the rubber meets the road. Here are some things to consider as you implement your intervention.

- Establish and document clear protocols for the implementation of your intervention. Your intervention documentation should be sufficiently detailed to allow you to pass the intervention process off to a colleague and allow them to implement the intervention exactly as you want it without your help.

- If your intervention is running for more than a couple of weeks, you should create a plan to allow for ongoing fidelity monitoring. You need to check in periodically to ensure that you are delivering the intervention as it was designed. Think of your educational intervention like a medical intervention; you want to know if it works as prescribed, and if it isn't being delivered correctly, you won't know for sure that it worked.

- Put systems in place to ensure that your control group remains your control group. They should be continuing with life as usual and should not have access to any part of the intervention during your experimental phase. This is a common pitfall for action research projects because as educators, we get excited when things start to work, and we want to spread the wealth fast. Remember that your goal is to prove whether the intervention is working or not, and to do so, you must maintain clear boundaries.

6	Gather your post-intervention data.

After allowing your intervention sufficient time to work, it is time to gather your post-intervention data. Deploy your evaluation protocols as you did before the start of the intervention. Essentially, you're going to replicate the processes you used during your baseline data collection in exactly the same way. This will give you two parallel sets of data that you can explore.

CHOOSE YOUR PATH

If your intervention phase went smoothly, and you didn't experience any hiccups, you are now ready to begin your data analysis. Turn to page 73 to learn how to use descriptive statistics to understand your data.

If your intervention phase had some bumps along the road, consider selecting a new batch of participants and running your experiment again. If you decide this is necessary, return to page 45 to start again.

Quasi-Experimental Design

Quasi-experimental designs seek to determine the impact of an intervention by comparing the performance of two groups—a control group and an intervention group. During the course of the study, the control group will go about business as usual while the intervention group receives an intervention. In a quasi-experimental study, the experimenter deploys the intervention using previously assigned groups. In education, these groups are usually classrooms or schools.

Quasi-experimental studies are common in education because researchers have quick and ready access to previously assigned groups of students. This type of study is less rigorous than an RCT due to the prevalence of confounding factors—or elements that may influence the outcome of the study. A lot goes into why Johnny is assigned to Mr. Napier's or Ms. Stein's classroom. Students are rarely randomly assigned to their teacher. By using these previously assigned groups to study an intervention, the researcher is unable to account for the various differences between the two classrooms.

Let's say that you want to conduct an experiment using Mr. Campbell's class and Ms. Foster's class. Mr. Campbell has been assigned all the students with individual education plans (IEPs) because he is dual certified to teach both fifth grade and special education. That extra certification is a confounding factor because he likely has skills that Ms. Foster may not have. Those skills will influence the way he manages his classroom, communicates with students, and ultimately administers the intervention during your experiment. Those changes, in turn, will influence the outcome of your experiment.

Practitioner researchers shouldn't feel discouraged from performing quasi-experimental studies due to the presence of confounding factors. In fact, very few practitioner researchers will have the ability to control group assignment and fully remove confounding factors from their project. Instead, practitioner researchers should be prepared to account for confounding factors during their data analysis and discussion. They should apply local contextual knowledge about the two groups and think through how local conditions may have influenced their study.

To conduct a quasi-experimental study in your classroom, follow these steps:

1	Identify your intervention and select your study participants.

If you haven't done so already, now is the time to determine which intervention you will be deploying to try to solve your problem of practice. You should have a good idea of which types of interventions may improve your situation based on the literature review that you conducted earlier.

Once you have selected your intervention, you will need to identify your study participants. Take a look at the participants available to you. Ideally, you will want to select two groups that are relatively similar. The groups should be about the same size, feature participants with roughly the same demographic makeup, and, if they are students, be performing at about the same level. If you see clear confounding factors, such as the dual certification issue mentioned above, try to see if there is another available comparison group to include in your experiment.

Finally, you will need to determine which group will be your control group and which group will be your intervention group. Choose the group with which you will be most successful at implementing your intervention with fidelity.

2	Identify/create your evaluation instrument(s).

Before you can begin your study, you need to identify and/or create your evaluation instruments. Your evaluation instruments are the tools you will use to gather the data necessary to determine if your intervention provided the desired outcome. Here are a few important considerations when selecting your evaluation instrument.

- Whenever possible, try to select a previously established evaluation instrument. A high quality independently developed instrument helps to ensure that the results of your study are measured accurately. These previously designed instruments could be standardized tests, published surveys, assessments included within a curriculum, standardized classroom observation instruments, or something similar.

- If you are seeking to evaluate the impact of a program or curriculum that includes evaluation instruments, try to find a different evaluation instrument that aligns with your study objectives. If you rely on the evaluation instruments housed within a packaged intervention, you may be assessing a student's ability to achieve within the program and not necessarily whether the student has achieved in an outcome aligned to the underlying learning target.

- If you plan to use a survey to measure changes in behavior or perception, the research literature may help you identify commonly used and respected surveys that already exist in the field. Before using a survey, contact the author to ask for permission, and be sure to cite their work when you present about your project.

- If you are creating your own instrument from scratch, take care to ensure that it is both valid and reliable. You could pilot your instrument on a small group of individuals who are not part of your study by administering your instrument twice with about a month in between. You can use a t-test (see page 86) to see if the two administrations were statistically similar. You should also have a team of colleagues review your instrument to see if they think it accurately assesses the intended outcome.

3	Collect some baseline data.

To understand how the performance of your participants has changed after the intervention, you must measure where they are before they begin to receive the intervention. This is called baseline data. Before you begin your study, take time to collect detailed demographic data and baseline assessment data on each participant.

Demographic data is an important component that will help you better understand the impact of the intervention on your participants in the end. This is especially important if you have students from a variety of identities or school-created labels (such as special education or low-income labels). Take time to think about all the various demographic elements you could collect on your participants and gather that information up front. It is easier to get this information from your participants at the beginning than to try to go back and collect demographic information after the study has concluded.

You should also deploy your previously selected evaluation instrument and gather some baseline data. Depending on your project, this baseline data collection may include administering your evaluation protocol in its entirety as a pre-test, or it may involve gathering previously collected data (such as behavior data, attendance data, or standardized assessment data) from an existing information system.

The last step before you begin to implement your intervention is to check for baseline equivalency. During this process, you will want to take a careful look at the data for your intervention and control groups to see how similar they are. If your group is large and you have properly performed a randomization protocol, your two groups should be similar. If your groups are not similar, you could run your randomization protocol again. If you ran a full group randomization and ended up with two very unbalanced groups, you could try switching to a stratified random assignment protocol. Whatever you do, do not manually move participants from one group to another to achieve balance. Doing so will undo your random assignment and introduce bias into your study.

4	Implement your intervention.

Having established your intervention, selected your participants, randomly sorted them into groups, and gathered some baseline data, you are now ready to perform your intervention! This is where the rubber meets the road. Here are some things to consider as you implement your intervention.

- Establish and document clear protocols for the implementation of your intervention. Your intervention documentation should be sufficiently detailed to allow you to pass the intervention process off to a colleague and allow them to implement the intervention exactly as you want it without your help.

- If your intervention is running for more than a couple of weeks, you should create a plan to allow for ongoing fidelity monitoring. You need to check in periodically to ensure that you are delivering the intervention as it was designed. Think of your educational intervention like a medical intervention; you want to know if it works as prescribed, and if it isn't being delivered correctly, you won't know for sure that it worked.

Put systems in place to ensure that your control group remains your control group. They should be continuing with life as usual and should not have access to any part of the intervention during your experimental phase. This is a common pitfall for action research projects because as educators, we get excited when things start to work, and we want to spread the wealth fast. Remember that your goal is to prove whether the intervention is working or not, and to do so, you must maintain clear boundaries.

5	Gather your post-intervention data.

After allowing your intervention sufficient time to work, it is time to gather your post-intervention data. Deploy your evaluation protocols as you did before the start of the intervention. Essentially, you're going to replicate the processes you used during your baseline data collection in exactly the same way. This will give you two parallel sets of data that you can explore.

CHOOSE YOUR PATH

If your intervention phase went smoothly and you didn't experience any hiccups, you are now ready to begin your data analysis. Turn to page 73 to learn how to use descriptive statistics to understand your data.

If your intervention phase had some bumps along the road, consider selecting a new batch of participants and running your experiment again. If you decide this is necessary, return to page 51 and repeat the steps to run your experiment again.

Single-Case Design

Single-case designs are those in which the researcher wants to understand the impact of an intervention on a single student. These studies are sometimes called ABA or ABAB studies because they are conducted in distinct phases. During the first phase, an A phase, no intervention is deployed, and baseline data is collected by the researcher. Baseline data is collected at regular intervals, usually daily. During the B phase, also called the intervention phase, an intervention is deployed, while the research continues to collect the same data at the same intervals. Finally, the intervention is removed, and a third set of data is collected. This is the second A phase, sometimes called the reversal phase.

The idea is pretty straightforward. You collect baseline data so that we can later compare that data to data collected during the intervention phase. If your intervention is working, you should see a positive change in the desired outcome. You then remove the intervention and continue collecting data to see if the intervention has created long-term changes to the outcome or if it must stay in place in order to help the student maintain the desired outcome.

This type of study helps the researcher understand how an intervention impacts the outcomes on a single pupil. The analysis can help measure the impact of a more targeted intervention and determine if the intervention has a long-term or short-term impact. When multiple single-case studies are performed using the same intervention, they begin to form a body of research that can help future educators choose effective interventions for their individual students.

To conduct a single-case design study in your classroom, follow these steps:

| 1 | Identify a single study participant and a desired outcome. |

Single-case studies are designed to be conducted using one subject for whom you wish to change a specific outcome. Think about the various people you serve through your position. Is there a student who is regularly off-task and disruptive? Maybe a supervisee who is regularly late to work? Or a behavior you would like to see exhibited differently from a kiddo in your math class?

Select your study subject and clearly define the desired outcome you would like to see.

| 2 | Identify an intervention. |

Spend some time reflecting on the desired outcome you identified in the previous step. Combine your reflections with the knowledge you acquired during your literature review. Select an intervention that you can deploy that you think would help your subject achieve the desired outcome. Before you begin your experiment, make sure you have fully wrapped your head around the intervention and have secured all the necessary materials to implement it.

| 3 | Collect baseline data. |

Begin your study by collecting baseline data. This is the A phase, or baseline phase, of your single-case design. Select a data element that is aligned to your desired outcome and document that element at regular time intervals. For example, let's say that you have a student who is regularly disruptive during your third period English class; he likes to get out of his seat and wander around the classroom. For the next ten school days, count the number of times he gets out of his seat and keep a record. Set up a spreadsheet like the one below to begin tracking your baseline data.

Model Spreadsheet for Collecting Single-Case Data

	A	B	C
1	**Date**	**Phase**	**Category**
2	08/01/22	A1	9
3	08/02/22	A1	8
4	08/03/22	A1	11

4	**Implement your intervention and continue collecting data.**

After you have a sufficient baseline data set, begin to implement your intervention. You are entering your first B phase, or your intervention phase. As you implement the intervention, continue collecting the same data elements at the same time intervals as before.

Model Spreadsheet for Collecting Single-Case Data

	A	B	C
1	**Date**	**Phase**	**Category**
2	08/11/22	B1	5
3	08/12/22	B1	6
4	08/13/22	B1	4

5	**Stop your intervention and continue collecting data.**

Now let's see if your intervention has led to a lasting change toward your desired outcome. This is your second A phase, or reversal phase. Stop the intervention but continue collecting the same data elements at the same time intervals.

Model Spreadsheet for Collecting Single-Case Data

	A	B	C
1	**Date**	**Phase**	**Category**
2	08/21/22	A2	7
3	08/22/22	A2	9
4	08/23/22	A2	8

6   Optional: Re-implement your intervention and continue collecting data.

Take a moment to look at your raw data. If you notice a slight change in the data during your reversal phase, you may decide to reimplement the intervention. If you do so, you should continue to collect the same data element at the same time intervals as before. This is your second B phase, or your second intervention phase. You may determine that a second intervention phase is not necessary—that is completely up to you.

Model Spreadsheet for Collecting Single-Case Data

	A	B	C
1	**Date**	**Phase**	**Category**
2	08/31/22	B2	3
3	09/01/22	B2	2
4	09/02/22	B2	4

CHOOSE YOUR PATH

If your intervention phase went smoothly and you didn't experience any hiccups, you are now ready to begin your data analysis. Turn to page 91 to learn how to begin your data analysis.

If your intervention phase had some bumps along the road, consider selecting a new participant(s) and running your experiment again. If you decide this is necessary, return to page 57 and repeat the steps to run your experiment again.

Descriptive and Correlational Study Designs

Descriptive studies are those that seek to report on the current state of a phenomenon. Correlational studies are those that seek to measure the relationship between variables. While these two research designs differ in their underlying purpose, the steps for establishing and performing both types of studies are the same, so we will explore them together here.

Remember that neither descriptive nor correlational studies can be used to determine causality. That is to say that we cannot use these study designs to suggest that one variable caused or influenced a phenomenon with certainty. Rather, we can use these study designs to help us understand the nuances of a given circumstance. These designs are sometimes called "observational studies" because the researcher is reporting their observations based on their collected data and without manipulating the variables as one does in an RCT or quasi-experimental study.

Descriptive and correlational study designs are useful when practitioner researchers have access to a large volume of archival or survey data, and they want to report on a phenomenon from a historical perspective or document relationships between two variables. Descriptive studies usually deploy descriptive statistics, such as the mean, median, mode, range, or standard deviation and rely on those measures to report in an unbiased way. Correlational studies may also report some or all of these descriptive statistics, but they will also report on the correlation coefficient.

To conduct a descriptive or correlational study in your classroom, follow these steps:

1	Identify the variables you will need to understand before you can describe a given phenomenon.

Descriptive and correlational study designs focus on understanding existing variables in relation to a phenomenon. As such, the first step in successfully completing either type of study is to consider the variables that you will need to examine. Think about the phenomenon you have chosen to study and begin to list the various elements that you think may describe the phenomenon. Try to create as comprehensive a list as possible during this stage. It is easier to remove unnecessary data later than to go back and find missing variables at the end of your study.

You should also consider the appropriate time periods which you may need to review. For example, if you want to understand the impact of a decision made five years ago, then you probably need seven to ten years of historical data in order to understand the circumstances prior to the decision, in the year of the decision, and in the years following the decision.

2	Gather relevant archival data.

Take the list you have created and begin to gather relevant archival data. Consider the wide variety of archival data sources available to you. There may be relevant data housed in archives within your institution, within your state systems, or within federal systems. Here are a few places to look for archival data:

- Start with your local system: School systems usually maintain some type of student information system (SIS). An SIS is a database in which all relevant data points for students are housed. They usually include directory information (addresses, phone numbers, etc.), demographic information (race/ethnicity, gender, identification for special education, etc.), behavior data (attendance, referrals, consequences, etc.), and achievement data (grades, standardized assessment scores, etc.). Your system may have one unified SIS, or it may deploy multiple systems which each collect a specific type of data. Talk to your system administrators if you need help accessing archival data housed within your system.

- State School Report Cards: The Every Student Succeeds Act of 2015 (ESSA) requires each state to maintain a publicly accessible school report card (SRC). These report cards should have a wide variety of student information. Under the ESSA, states are required to update their SRC annually, and they must include the following data elements:
    - A description of, and results from, the state's accountability system;
    - Student academic achievement as measured through the administration of federally required standardized assessments;
    - Graduation rates;
    - The number of English Learners and their progress toward achieving English proficiency;
    - Measures of student progress toward achieving state-designated goals;
    - All information required by the Civil Rights Data Collection (discussed below);
    - Information on educator qualifications;
    - Information on students with disabilities;
    - Results from the National Assessment of Educational Progress (NAEP; discussed below);
    - Information on post-secondary enrollment; and
    - A variety of financial data, such as per-pupil expenditures and spending information for federal programs like the school improvement fund.

- Civil Rights Data Collection: If you are interested in studying behavioral outcomes or examining equity issues either within your system, state, or nation, the Civil Rights Data Collection (CRD) is a good place to start. States are required to annually report a wide variety of information, such as behavior referrals and resolutions, access to high quality course work, and teacher credentialing to the US Department of Education. You can access this information at https://ocrdata.ed.gov.

- National Assessment of Educational Progress: The National Assessment of Educational Progress (NAEP) is a nationwide standardized assessment administered annually in the United States. Billed as "the Nation's Report Card," the assessment is given in most states to fourth and eighth graders in the areas of reading, mathematics, and science. Some states have expanded their NAEP administrations to include the arts, civics, geography, economics, technology and engineering, US history, and/or writing. You can access national, state, school, or system-level NAEP results at https://nces.ed.gov/nationsreportcard.

- National Center for Education Statistics: Another great place to look for archival education data is the National Center for Education Statistics (NCES). This congressionally funded center maintains a variety of surveys and programs to help researchers understand what's going on in the nation's school systems. Many of the NCES surveys contain data going back to the early 2000s, making it a great place to look for long-term changes. You can access data from the NCES website at https://nces.ed.gov.

3	Create and administer a survey (if necessary).

As you gather your data, you may find that there is a gap in the archival data available to you. If this is the case, it may be appropriate for you to develop and administer a survey to collect the required data. There are a few kinds of survey instruments that may be appropriate for deployment in a descriptive or correlational study.

If you are lacking specific data points that you think school or system leaders may be able to provide to you, then an information-gathering survey might be a good option. In this type of survey, you will simply want to list the missing data elements and ask the leader to fill in the gaps. This type of survey is relatively straightforward and works great if you are seeking simple numerical responses.

If you want to survey to find information related to changes in behavior or perception, your best bet is to identify a previously validated and administered survey in the literature. The literature review that you have already conducted should have helped you to identify commonly used survey instruments related to your question. Before using a survey, contact the author of those surveys to ask for permission, and be sure to cite their work when you present about your project.

If you are creating your own instrument from scratch, take care to ensure that it is both valid and reliable. You could pilot your instrument on a small group of individuals who are not part of your study by administering your instrument twice with about a month in between. You can use a t-test (see page 86) to see if the two administrations were statistically similar. You should also have a team of colleagues review your instrument to see if they think it accurately assesses the intended outcome.

4	Gather your collected data neatly and in one place.

Before you end your data collection phase, take time to gather your data neatly in one place. You are going to need to perform many calculations to accurately describe the history of a phenomenon or to examine the correlations between variables. Take time at this stage to make sure that your files are neatly stored, that your data is easily accessible, and that you haven't duplicated any data within your spreadsheets.

Once your files are tidy, duplicate them to create a backup set of files. This will ensure that you always have access to your originally sourced data as you begin to manipulate the data in the next step.

CHOOSE YOUR PATH

Once you have gathered all the necessary data, turn to page 73 to learn how to use descriptive statistics to understand your data.

Qualitative Study Design

Qualitative study designs are those in which a researcher seeks to understand how a phenomenon has changed over time and/or how it has impacted a community. Under this framework, practitioner researchers primarily use interviews or document analysis to gather information before deploying coding methodologies to summarize the work.

Qualitative research is often treated as a field unto itself. It encompasses a wide variety of techniques and analytic methods. Within the context of action research, practitioner researchers are often too limited in their time and resources to focus on any one qualitative ideology and deploy their study with the necessary rigors it prescribes. This section seeks to provide the practitioner researcher with the steps necessary to complete a qualitative analysis within the context of school improvement, but it is important that readers understand that this section does not represent a complete and thorough discussion of the field of qualitative research.

To conduct a qualitative study in your school, follow these steps:

1	**Identify the archival documents and/or interview candidates necessary to help you understand your selected phenomenon.**

As qualitative studies consist of interviews or document review, it seems only logical that the first step in the process is to identify the necessary documents or interview candidates. Depending on the phenomenon you have chosen, you may need to review a wide range of documents, interview a wide range of candidates, or perhaps do a little of both. Here are some things to consider as you build your list.

- If your study revolves around a policy decision, take time to find all the relevant archival information about that policy. This should include both current and historical versions of the policy or copies of other policies that impacted the development of the policy you're studying (such as laws that impacted the implementation of a regulation), as well as any testimony or public comments made by policymakers during the development of the policy.

- If your study involves reviewing student work samples, curriculum, or other forms of written documentation, be sure that the sample that you collect is thorough and accurately represents the phenomenon you wish to study. For example, if you are studying the impact of a writing lesson that you pulled from an established curriculum, you must use student work samples that were derived from that lesson if you want to understand how the lesson impacted the quality of their writing.

- When considering interview candidates, it is important to identify those individuals most impacted by the phenomenon you're studying. Be sure that you are spending time with carefully selected individuals who can provide you with good insight into the phenomenon. Expand your list to include those impacted in both positive and negative ways and those charged with implementing or overseeing a phenomenon. It is easy for researchers to focus their interviews only on those they perceive to be negatively impacted by a phenomenon or to vilify those in positions of authority. Be sure to check your bias at the door and investigate your phenomenon deeply and from all sides. Remember, you're a researcher not a reporter.

2	Collect archival documents (if necessary).

Having identified the documents you need to review, the next step is to collect those archival documents. Here are some things to consider as you gather your documents:

- Begin your search by accessing documents that are already available to you. This could be things like student work samples, newspaper articles, or policy documents.

- Enlist the support of a research librarian to gain access to historical perspectives on policy documents. Older documents are likely accessible through your local library and their larger interlibrary loan network.

Consider filing a request with a government official. Most government documents are open to public access. This can be accomplished through a Freedom of Information Act Request (FOIA). These requests are sometimes called Open Records Requests (ORR) by state and local governments. A representative of any government agency should be able to assist you with this process.

3	Develop and implement an interview protocol (if necessary).

If you have decided that your project requires interviewing, the next step is to develop your interview protocols and conduct your interviews. While there are many interview protocols available to practitioner researchers, I suggest deploying the semi-structured interview protocol. In this protocol, you will craft a series of predetermined questions which you will ask each interviewee in the same way. Then you may ask specific follow-up questions that may differ from interview to interview.

Interviews are extremely personal and can put the interviewee in a vulnerable position. Before beginning your interview process, please revisit our discussion on research ethics (pg. 22) and research biases (pg. 24). You should begin each interview with a standardized statement that gives the participant an opportunity to opt out. Here is a model statement:

> Thank you for agreeing to participate in this research interview. I am trying to understand how [your phenomenon] has impacted [you/your community]. Today, I will be conducting a semi-structured interview, which means that I have some predetermined questions but may ask follow-up questions as we engage in our conversation. When I'm done, this transcript will be combined with the transcripts of other interviews for analysis. Your comments today are confidential and will be fully anonymized before being presented. Do you still consent to participating in this interview?

Your interview protocol should include clear steps for maintaining a confidential environment and for anonymizing any information before reporting. Your final project is not a newspaper article; it is generally considered to be inappropriate to refer to individual participants by name in qualitative research reports.

You should also plan to record and transcribe your interviews. This will ensure that you have accurate information to code later. Do not rely on your own handwritten notes.

4	**Organize files and transcripts so that they can be easily analyzed.**

The final step in the process is to organize your files and transcripts so that they can be analyzed. If you haven't already, convert any audio or video files into verbatim transcripts of your interviews. Make sure that you have all your documents sorted into folders and keep a master list of all the documents you plan to review. I also recommend keeping a duplicate copy of each document so that you always have a clean original version to return to.

CHOOSE YOUR PATH

Once you have completed gathering your documents and transcribing your interviews, turn to page 97 to learn how to code your data.

Calculating Descriptive Statistics

If your study involved collecting numerical data on your study participants, then the first step to your analysis is to summarize your data using descriptive statistics. Descriptive statistics help you summarize and describe a distribution of scores. This is an important step that you will want to perform on each set of scores you collected regardless of your study design. This section will teach you how to calculate and interpret key descriptive statistics using standard spreadsheet software functions. This section is also supported by instructional videos which can be found at https://www.matthewbcourtney.com/actionresearch.

Mean

The mean is the statistical average of a range of scores. You calculate the mean by adding up all the individual scores and then dividing the sum by the total number of all scores. You have probably performed this calculation hundreds of times when assigning grades to students at the end of the semester. The mean is the most commonly used descriptive statistic as it is easily calculated and easily understood by most people.

The mean is a valuable statistic and is often the first statistic calculated when summarizing data. In education, it is usually used to compare outcomes between groups, to compare the past outcomes to the current outcomes within a single group, or to communicate about outcomes to stakeholders. It is also a prerequisite to many more rigorous statistical calculations deployed by analysts seeking to make inferences about a set of data.

One downside to the mean is that it is heavily swayed by outliers or skewed data. An outlier is when you have a single data point that is far above or far below the rest of the data. Skewed data are when your data are asymmetrical, meaning that the data points are falling at irregular and unexpected intervals. If you have a few students who scored far above or far below the rest of the students, the mean will be skewed in that direction. Remember teasing the "curve busters" in your classes in high school? Those students "broke the curve" because they scored so far above the rest of us that the average on the test was higher than it should have been–discouraging our teachers from granting bonus points across the board.

In your spreadsheet software, you can calculate the mean using the **AVERAGE** function. The syntax for this function is below. Simply type "**=AVERAGE**" into an empty cell, followed by the range of cells for which you want to know the average.

<u>Syntax for the Average Function</u>

=AVERAGE(range)
range the selection of cells, usually a column, that contains the data that you want to summarize

Median

The median is the score in the exact middle of your distribution when you line them all up in order. If you have an even number of scores, then the median is the average of the two scores in the middle. You can only calculate the median if you have ordinal data–that is, data that can be placed in a logical order, such as a test score.

The median is a close cousin to the mean, and they work and play together well. In a perfectly distributed set of scores, the mean and median should be the same because they will both be in the exact middle of the distribution. Unfortunately, a perfectly distributed set of scores is a freak of nature that almost never happens in real life. As such, the relationship between the mean and median is important because it can give you a feel for the skew of your data.

The skew describes which way your data leans. If the median is higher than the mean, then the data are said to "skew to the left" or to have a negative skew. That means that the outliers or potential disparities in your data are on the lower end of the spectrum. When your median is lower than the mean, the opposite is true. These data "skew to the right," or have a positive skew, meaning that the outliers or disparities in your data are on the upper end of the spectrum.

The relationship between the mean and the median are helpful when seeking to understand the nuances of your data. When using these statistics to help you make decisions, they can help you quickly see if your students are performing as expected (statistically) or if there may be circumstances influencing their outcomes (causing skew).

Spreadsheet packages make calculating the median very easy. The syntax simply involves typing the name of the test and selecting a range of cells to summarize. The **MEDIAN** function will return the middle number in a distribution with an odd number of scores or the average of the two middle numbers in an even number of scores. Simply type "**=MEDIAN**" followed by the range in parentheses.

<u>Syntax for the Median Function</u>

=MEDIAN(range)	
Range	the selection of cells, usually a column, that contains the data that you want to summarize

Mode

The mode is simply the number, or numbers, that occur most frequently in a distribution of scores. The mode is best applied to categorical data and can be used to easily explain which category has the highest number of inputs. A distribution of scores may be unimodal, containing only one mode, bi-modal, containing two modes, or multi-modal, containing more than two modes. It can also have no mode at all. By examining the mode, you can quickly spot clusters in your data that may contain useful information.

Mode can be a very useful score when you want to examine your total student population a little more closely. For example, let's say your data contains the number of behavior referrals given out at your school during the last school year, and you have found that the average number of behavior referrals is twenty-five. That is a lot of referrals, but that doesn't mean that most of your students had twenty-five referrals. Remember that the mean is easily swayed by outliers and discrepancies. If you calculate the mode, you will likely find that most students had either zero or one referral for the whole school year. This discovery tells a different, more complete story of your data.

Spreadsheet packages usually offer three versions of the mode function. The first, most straightforward function, is **MODE**. This function will return either a single mode, or if there is no mode, it will return an N/A. The mode formula has two variants: **MODE.SNGL** and **MODE.MULTI**. The first will return a single mode if the data has only a single mode. If there are multiple modes, **MODE.SNGL** will return the first mode it finds, usually the lowest. For a distribution with multiple modes, **MODE.MULTI** will return each mode in a distribution. If you are faced with a large data set, my advice is to always use the **MODE.MULTI** function. The syntax for all three variants can be found below.

=MODE(range)
range the selection of cells, usually a column, that contains the data that you want to summarize

=MODE.SNGL(range)
range the selection of cells, usually a column, that contains the data that you want to summarize

=MODE.MULTI(range)
range the selection of cells, usually a column, that contains the data that you want to summarize

Range

The range is a measure of dispersion. It is the most straightforward of the descriptive statistics mentioned in this section. It tells the reader how far apart the highest and lowest scores are in a distribution. This is important because it gives context to your study outcomes and helps the reader understand the importance of changes within your study. Calculating the range in a spreadsheet package is simple. To calculate the range, you will subtract the function **MIN** from the function **MAX** as is demonstrated in the table below.

Syntax for the Range Formula

=MAX(range)-MIN(range)
range the selection of cells, usually a column, that contains the data that you want to summarize

Standard Deviation

The standard deviation is a more rigorous measure of dispersion as it applies some heavy math to the situation. A low standard deviation indicates that most of the scores are clustered around the mean while a high standard deviation indicates that the scores are more spread out. A standard deviation of zero, for example, would mean that all scores are exactly the same.

Standard deviations group scores around the mean and exist along a bell curve. In a perfect distribution, 68.2 percent of your students will be within one standard deviation of the mean, 34.1 percent above the mean and 34.1 percent below the mean. As we get further away from the mean, we should see fewer students falling into the various standard deviation categories. For example, 13.6 percent of students should fall within two standard deviations of the mean, 2.1 percent should fall within three standard deviations, and 0.1 percent should fall within four standard deviations. This phenomenon is depicted in the image on the next page.

So what does all that mean? Consider the standard IQ test, which has an average of 100 and a standard deviation of 15. We can assume that if we gave a standard IQ test to our students, 68.2 percent of our students would score within a range of 85 and 115 points, that is, 15 points on either side of the mean. These are our typically developing students. We can assume that 13.6 percent of our students would score within two standard deviations, meaning either between 70 and 85 points on the low end or 115 and 130 points on the high end. These are our upper and lower performing students. We can continue in this manner, adding or subtracting 15 each time, to identify our students who might require special education or gifted and talented services.

Normal Distribution with Standard Deviation Markers

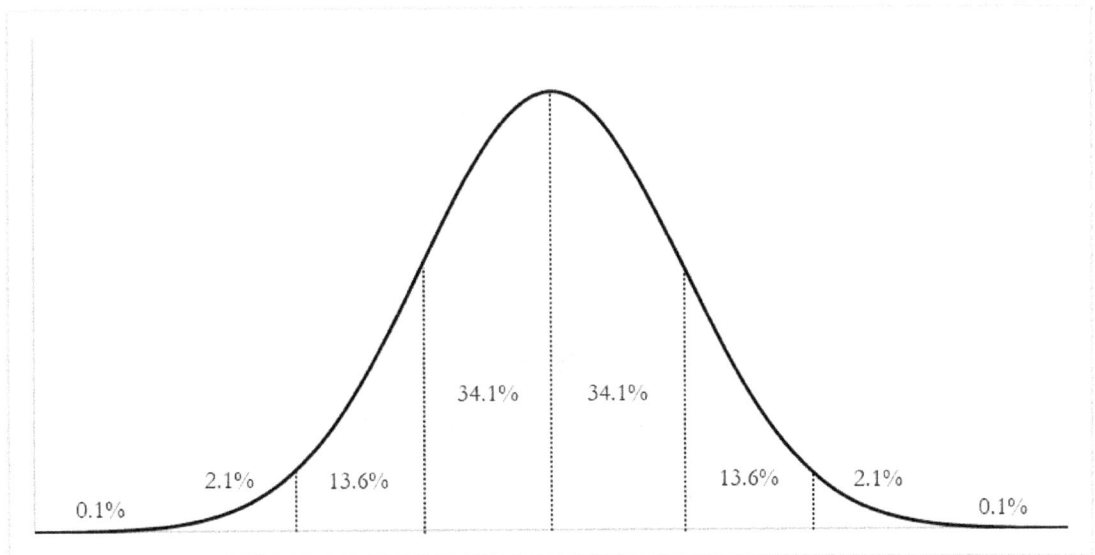

34.1%   34.1%

2.1%   13.6%   13.6%   2.1%

0.1%   0.1%

While the IQ model uses nice round numbers, this will rarely be the case in real life. You can use the standard deviation for a variety of purposes, such as identifying students for remediation or acceleration or examining the equity of your multi-tiered systems of support (MTSS) model. Standard deviation is also frequently reported alongside the outcomes of inferential statistics.

To calculate the standard deviation in spreadsheet software, you must deploy the standard deviation function. There are usually two versions of the standard deviation function available in most software packages. The **STDEV.P** function calculates the standard deviation for an entire population; hence the "p" at the end of its name. You will use this function when you want to examine the standard deviation for an entire population, such as all the students that you teach. If you are examining the standard deviation of samples extracted from your whole population, then you use the **STDEV.S** function; the "s" stands for sample. The math behind this function varies slightly in that it accounts for the fact that you are only analyzing a small portion of your overall sample. The syntax for each function can be found below.

Syntax for the Standard Deviation, Population Function

=STDEV.P(range)
range   the selection of cells, usually a column, that contains the data that you want to summarize

Syntax for the Standard Deviation, Sample Function

=STDEV.S(range)
range   the selection of cells, usually a column, that contains the data that you want to summarize

Pivot Tables and Data Disaggregation

Depending on the type of data you have collected, it may be appropriate to disaggregate your data by various sub-populations. Data disaggregation is the process of sorting data into groups to allow you to compare performance among those groups. Elements of data disaggregation can also be layered on top of one another, allowing you to examine outcomes for students who may be part of more than one group. This is called intersectionality.

Let's think about this in context. If you know that the average performance on an assessment is 60.0, you will have a general idea of the overall performance of your group. If you can sort that group by gender, you may learn that male students scored 68.7 on average, while female students scored 50.7. Does that change the way you think about your data? What if we layer special education designations on top of that and find out that females without a special education designation scored 72.4, while females with a special education designation scored 29.0? See how much more detail you can start to uncover?

In a spreadsheet package, the fastest way to calculate descriptive statistics while also disaggregating the data by multiple levels is by creating a pivot table. Pivot tables are interactive tables that are built into most spreadsheet platforms. Essentially, a pivot table allows you to perform all the same functions presented in this section by simply dragging and dropping variables into a table-building wizard. While each spreadsheet package has its own variations on how a pivot table functions, they generally follow a few basic principles.

Creating a new pivot table is easy. Generally, spreadsheet programs will have a button that says something to the effect of "Create a Pivot Table." When you click this button, you will be asked to select a series of data points to feed into your pivot table. Usually it is best to select the entire data set that you intend to examine. When you do so, a new worksheet will open within your existing spreadsheet file. This is where you will build out the rest of your pivot table.

Unlike a basic spreadsheet table, which you build by typing functions or formulas, a pivot table is built using an editing window. The editor window consists of five parts. First, the editor will include a list of fields or variables. This list is made up of the column titles from your original data worksheet. You will build out your pivot table by dragging those fields into one of the four pivot table elements: the rows, columns, values, and filters.

The elements are named sensibly. If you want to see a specific variable broken out into rows, you can drag it to the Rows element. If you want to see it in columns, you drag it to the Columns element. The Filter element will create a drop-down menu that allows you to see only a particular subset of your data, while the Values element is where you will place the key function you want to understand. It takes at least two elements to build a pivot table, but you can use all four elements to build hyper-specific outputs.

Pivot tables can be a head-scratcher when you first start out, but once you get into them, they can save you a lot of time. The best way to learn them is simply to upload some data, create a pivot table, and start clicking around. The individual screens and options for pivot tables vary with each software package, which is why they are not discussed in detail here. I have included some additional resources and walk-through videos to help you learn to use pivot tables in the online videos that accompany this book. You can access them at http://www.matthewbcourtney.com/actionresearch.

Online Tools

In addition to the time-tested techniques discussed above, the online supplements for this book include two interactive tools to help you comb through and summarize your data. The first is called the "Distribution Analysis Tool," and it can be accessed at https://www.matthewbcourtney.com/dat. To use the tool, simply upload your spreadsheet as a .CSV file and select the column you want to summarize from the dropdown menu. The tool will automatically summarize your distribution and create a report that includes the mean, median, mode, standard deviation, minimum, maximum, and range. It will also create a boxplot and a histogram to help you visualize your data more clearly.

The second tool is called the "Data Disaggregation Tool," and it can be accessed at https://www.matthewbcourtney.com/disaggregate. Like the tool mentioned above, you simply upload your spreadsheet as a .CSV file and select the columns you wish to analyze. The tool will create tables that disaggregate your data by one group and present the mean, median, mode, standard deviation, minimum, maximum, and range for each group. The tool also creates a boxplot that allows you to compare the outcomes for two groups at a glance. Each of the tools also include video instruction to help ensure your success.

CHOOSE YOUR PATH

If your study design requires you to compare the performance of two groups, turn to page 85 to learn how to use inferential statistics to compare two distributions of data.

If your study design requires you to describe the relationship between two variables, turn to page 81 to learn how to calculate the correlation coefficient.

If you have deployed a descriptive study design, then your data analysis procedure is complete! Turn to page 101 to learn how to make an evidence-informed decision.

Correlational Analysis

Correlation is a statistical measure that shows the strength of the relationship between two variables. One of the beautiful things about correlation is that it is extremely fast to calculate and super easy to interpret. Correlations exist on a range from negative one to positive one, with zero indicating that there is no correlation between the two variables. The correlation coefficient is denoted in a text with a lower-case r. A correlation of positive one means that there is a very strong relationship between two variables, while the opposite is true for a correlation of negative one.

The images on the next page help to demonstrate what each type of correlation would look like if you plotted the data points on a graph. The first image represents a negative correlation of $r = -0.99$. You can see that when Variable A is high, Variable B is low. The second image represents a null correlation of $r = 0.00$. You can see on this image that there is no clear relationship between the two variables. The final image represents a positive correlation of $r = 0.99$ and shows that Variable A and Variable B are closely related. When one is high, the other is high, and vice versa.

There is an important nuance to consider when using correlation to examine the relationships between variables. You have undoubtedly heard the phrase "correlation does not equal causation" at some point during your formal education. This is one of the most common proverbs in the world of statistical education. I've even seen it on T-shirts and ball caps! This phrase serves as a reminder that just because two variables are related doesn't mean that the first variable influenced the second variable.

Let's say that the variable "proficiency in reading" has a correlation of $+1.0$ with the variable "minutes of recess" in your dataset. This would indicate that students who had more minutes of recess also had higher reading outcomes. Just because the two variables may be positively correlated doesn't necessarily mean that more minutes of recess *caused* students to have higher reading outcomes. It could simply be a fluke. For this reason, we must be careful when drawing conclusions and making decisions based on the correlation between two variables.

Correlation Visualizations

Negative Correlation: r = -0.99

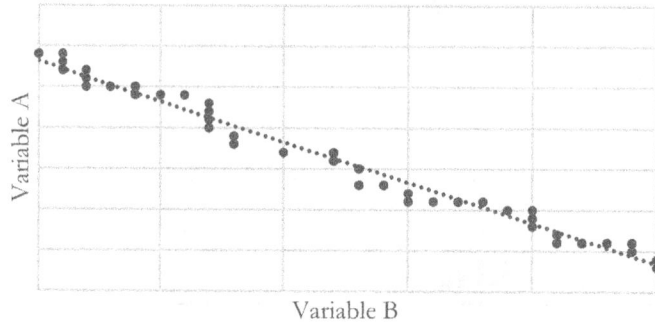

Variable A (vertical axis) vs Variable B (horizontal axis)

No Correlation: r = 0.00

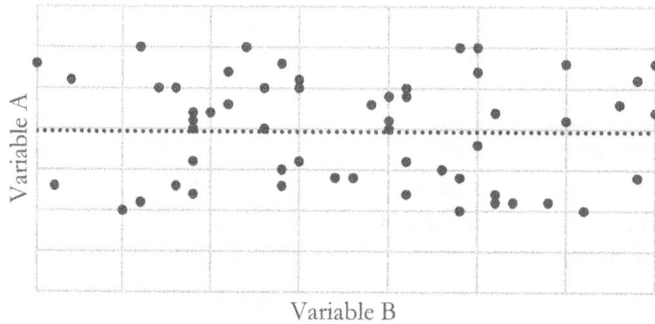

Variable A (vertical axis) vs Variable B (horizontal axis)

Positive Correlation: r = 0.99

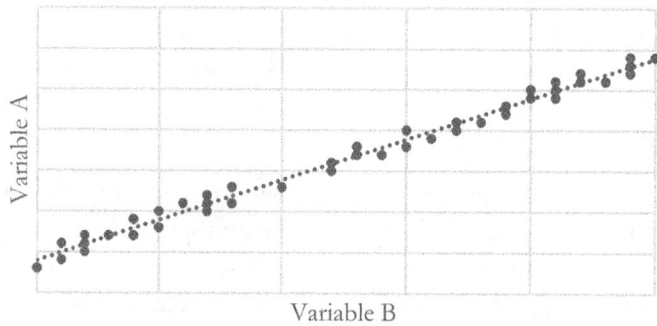

Variable A (vertical axis) vs Variable B (horizontal axis)

Even though the results are nuanced, calculating the correlation between two variables is still a valuable activity within the contexts of action research projects for a few reasons. First—it is easy and fast, which makes it a great step to include in a data analysis procedure. If there is no correlation between two variables, it is unlikely that there will be other statistical outcomes of significance between those two variables. You can save a little time by weeding through variables using correlation as a first step.

Next, correlation is an excellent measure of effect size. It is far easier to calculate than more formal measures of effect size, like Cohen's d (which we will discuss later), which involves calculating the mean of each variable and dividing it by the pooled standard deviation. If you have determined that a strategy deployed in one classroom produced a statistically significant outcome when compared to another classroom, the correlation may be a quick and easy way to help you express the size of the difference between those two outcomes.

Finally, correlations can help you spot instructional inequities. In a purely equitable world, there should be no correlation between demographic group and outcome—because one shouldn't be related to the other. We don't live in a purely equitable world, so calculating the correlations between various demographic groups is a useful activity for education leaders examining pockets of inequity. If you cannot see the inequity, then you cannot fix it. Dropping your data into a correlation matrix generator as part of your regular EDA procedure can help you quickly spot inequities and monitor changes as you seek to close the achievement gap.

To calculate the correlation between two distributions of data, you will use the **PEARSON** function. The **PEARSON** function returns the Pearson product-moment correlation between the two distributions of data that you select. Remember that the results of this test exist on a range of -1 to 1 where zero equals no correlation.

<u>Syntax for the PEARSON Function</u>

=PEARSON(range1, range2)
range1   the first selection of cells, usually a column, that contains the data that you want to examine **range2**   the second selection of cells, usually a column, that contains the data that you want to examine

One common way to review correlations for a large-scale set of data is to present it in a correlation matrix. A correlation matrix is a type of data visualization that shows the relationship between all the available variables in one spot. A decision-maker can then quickly spot very large or very small correlations for decision-making. A sample correlation matrix is presented below. You can see that the correlation between Variable One and Variable One is 1.00. That makes sense because they are the same thing; therefore, they should be exactly correlated. You can then see quickly that the correlation between Variable One and Variable Two is higher than those of Variables One and Three and Variables Two and Three.

Correlation Matrix Example

	A	B	C	D
1		Variable One	Variable Two	Variable Three
2	Variable One	1.00		
3	Variable Two	0.75	1.00	
4	Variable Three	0.02	0.25	1.00

Online Tools

As with the other techniques we've reviewed thus far, this book comes with access to an online tool to help you build correlation matrices with ease. The Correlation Matrix Generator can be accessed at https://matthewbcourtney.com/cor. When you upload your data as a .CSV file into the generator, it will read all of your variable headings for Row One of your spreadsheet and create a color-coded correlation matrix that can be saved as an image to your computer. The matrix will color code using shades of red and blue, with darker red colors representing stronger positive relationships and darker blue colors representing stronger negative relationships.

CHOOSE YOUR PATH

Now that you have completed your data analysis, turn to page 101 to learn how to make an evidence-informed decision.

Comparing Two Distributions

If your action research project involves collecting data in a pre-test/post-test format or comparing the outcomes of a control group to those of an intervention group, than you must look beyond descriptive statistics to understand the overall impact of your study. Differences in elements like mean or standard deviation may be helpful to observe, but to truly know how different the two distributions are, you must check for statistical and practical significance.

Statistical Significance

When talking about educational data, it is common for decision-makers to reference the statistical significance of a difference between two outcome variables. This measure is determined by deploying a technique called null-hypothesis testing, or NHT. Broadly speaking, in an NHT, the data analyst has two or more distributions of data that reflect differing variables or treatments. The analyst then deploys statistical tests to determine if the two distributions had statistically different outcomes. Common NHTs include the t-test and the Analysis of Variance (ANOVA). By deploying these tests, researchers can understand if the differences between two distributions of scores are due to an intervention or reflect a random chance.

For the purposes of this book, I am going to focus here solely on the t-test. If you have followed the path outlined in this book, then the t-test is the most appropriate null-hypothesis test for your project.

There are two types of t-test: the paired sample and the independent sample. In a paired-sample t-test, you compare the same group of data at two different times, such as in a pre-test and post-test outcome. In this instance, the two samples are paired; you have a pair of numbers for each student. If you have two different samples, such as post-test scores for control and intervention groups, you can compare them using an independent two-sample t-test. If the two data samples have the same number of scores, you can use the equal-variance t-test, and if they have different numbers, you use the unequal-variance t-test.

The t-test can also be either one-tailed or two-tailed. Run a one-tailed t-test if you want to know if the mean of one group is significantly higher than the other, and the two-tailed test if you want to check to see if the means are significantly higher or lower.

While a t-test can yield many different figures, the statistical significance of an outcome is commonly determined using the p-value. The p-value is the probability that an outcome occurred by random chance. The p-value is an oddly controversial value and one that is commonly discussed among statisticians and research scientists. If you want to get deep into the weeds, open your favorite search engine and type "p-value," and you will see what I'm talking about.

While scholars continue to debate the relevance and accuracy of the p-value, the generally accepted rules for interpreting a p-value have remained constant for decades. In short, the lower the p-value, the stronger the statistical significance. It is commonly accepted that the results of a statistical test are significant if the p-value is below 0.05 and strongly significant if it is below 0.01 or 0.001. You will always see the p-value reported along with statistical outcomes in educational research papers.

In a spreadsheet package, the **T.TEST** function allows you to quickly compare the means of two distributions of scores to determine if they are statistically significant. The **T.TEST** function requires four inputs. First, you must select the two distributions you wish to compare separated by a comma. Next, you must select the tails of the t-test. Set the tails argument to "1" if you want the t-test to use the one-tailed distribution or "2" if you want the t-test to use the two-tailed distribution. Finally, you must select one of the three t-test types. Set the type argument to "1" if you want to calculate a paired sample t-test, "2" if you want to calculate a two-sample t-test with equal variance, or "3" if you want to calculate a two-sample t-test with unequal variance. The result you see on the screen is your p-value.

<u>Syntax for the T.TEST Function</u>

=T.TEST(range1, range2, tails, type)	
range1	the first selection of cells, usually a column, that contains the data that you want to examine
range2	the second selection of cells, usually a column, that contains the data that you want to examine
tails	set to "1" if the t-test uses the one-tailed distribution or "2" if the t-test uses the two-tailed distribution
type	set to "1" if you want to calculate a paired-sample t-test, "2" if you want to calculate a two-sample with equal variance t-test, or "3" if you want to calculate a two-sample with unequal variance t-test

Practical Significance

When considering the impact of an educational intervention on your students, statistical significance isn't the end of the sentence. You should also seek to measure the practical significance of your outcomes. Practical significance helps you to understand the magnitude of the difference between two sets of scores.

Effect size is the most well-known measure of magnitude in education with the most common formula being Cohen's d. Effect size is calculated by dividing the difference between two means by the pooled standard deviation. If that formula sounds complicated, never fear. I am going to go through it step by step below.

To put effect size into layman's terms, the formula provides a standardized way to say that the average of group one is this far away from the average of group two. Effect size can also be used to examine the difference between pre-test and post-test scores. In that context, it provides a standardized way to say the group experienced this much change between test administrations.

Unlike statistical significance, the higher the effect size, the stronger the effect is determined to be. It is commonly accepted that an effect size is small when $d = 0.20$, medium when $d = 0.50$, and large when $d = 0.80$. Of course, you will rarely have an effect size that is exactly $d = 0.80$, so these numbers provide a rough guide to help you think about effect size results on a spectrum.

While effect size, and specifically Cohen's d, are growing extremely popular in education and in other scientific research fields, most spreadsheet packages do not include functions to calculate the effect size. Therefore, you must write a formula.

To start, you must first calculate the average, or mean, of your two distributions. You will do this using the **AVERAGE** function discussed in the section on descriptive statistics. Next, you need to use the **STDEV.P** function to calculate the standard deviation of each distribution. Finally, you need to know the total number of scores in your distribution. I recommend putting this information into a fresh table, like the one below.

Sample Spreadsheet Table

	A	B	C	D
1		Mean	Standard_Deviation	Count
2	Range 1	=AVERAGE(A:A)	=STDEV.P(A:A)	=COUNTA(A:A)
3	Range 2	=AVERAGE(B:B)	=STDEV.P(B:B)	=COUNTA(B:B)

Once you have this information, you are ready to calculate the pooled standard deviation. The formula for pooled standard deviation is below. It looks a little tricky, so let's break it down. We are going to add together the product of the adjusted count of range one and the squared standard deviation of range one with the product of the adjusted count of range two and the squared standard deviation of range two. You will then divide that by the adjusted count of all scores. Finally, calculate the square root of that number and you have the pooled standard deviation. Still confused? That's okay–just follow the formula below. That's why it's there.

Syntax for the Pooled Standard Deviation Formula

$$=SQRT(((n1-1)*SD1\char`^2+(n2-1)*SD2\char`^2)/(n1+n2-2))$$

n_1	the count of range 1
SD_1	the standard deviation of range 1
n_2	the count of range 2
SD_2	the standard deviation of range 2

Finally, to calculate the effect size, you simply subtract the average of range one from the average of range two, then divide by your newly calculated pooled standard deviation.

Syntax for the Effect Size Formula

$$=(M1-M2)/SDp$$

M_1	the mean (or average) of range 1
M_2	the mean (or average) of range 2
SDp	the pooled standard deviation

Online Tools

You can expedite the comparison of two distributions of scores using another online tool provided with this book. The tool is called the "Distribution Comparison Tool" and can be accessed at https://matthewbcourtney.com/dct. To use the tool, upload your data as a .CSV file, then select the appropriate distributions from the two drop-down menus on the screen. The tool will populate information on two tabs. Tab One will summarize your first distribution of scores, Tab Two will summarize your second distribution of score, and Tab Three will provide measures of statistical and practical significance. The tool will also generate visualizations that can help you better understand your outcomes.

CHOOSE YOUR PATH

Now that you have completed your data analysis, turn to page 101 to learn how to make an evidence-informed decision.

Single-Case Data Analysis

Single-case studies, those that examine the impact of an intervention on a single study participant, are conducted in phases. The data analysis procedure is conducted in phases too. To understand the impact of an intervention on a single subject, you first begin by summarizing each of the phases in your study, next you compare those phases, and finally you visualize the phases.

Summarize the Phases

The first step to successfully analyzing your single-case data is to summarize each of the phases using descriptive statistics. This is sometimes called the within-phase analysis. To complete this step, begin by calculating measures of central tendency for each phase in your study. The two measures of central tendency best applied in this context are mean and median. The mean is the statistical average of the data points, while the median represents the number in the exact middle of the distribution. Both statistics are easily calculated using spreadsheet software. The syntax for each is presented below.

<u>Syntax for the Average Function</u>

=AVERAGE(range)
range   the selection of cells, usually a column, that contains the data that you want to summarize

=MEDIAN(range)
range   the selection of cells, usually a column, that contains the data that you want to summarize

As you begin to examine your data, it can be helpful to build a simple table (like the one below) in your spreadsheet software to help you quickly see and compare the different scores. This will help you keep your data nice and tidy and will save you time later should you need to include tables in your paper or presentation.

Sample Phase Table

	A	B	C	D
1		A1	B1	A2
2	Mean	7.6	2.7	5.6
3	Median	7	2	5

This simple table can help us understand what our data is trying to say. We can see that the baseline average, collected during the A1 phase, is 7.6 with a median of 7. Both measures drop dramatically when we enter the intervention phase (B1), with an average of 2.7 and a median of 2. This suggests that our intervention had the desired effect. When we removed the intervention during the reversal phase (A2), both the average and the median go up slightly, but not to baseline levels. This suggests that our intervention continued to work a little bit even once it was no longer deployed.

Once you have the mean, you want to examine your data points to check for stability. The stability of the data describes the variation of individual data points from the mean. If most of your data points (80 to 90 percent) fall within fifteen percent of the mean, your data is considered to be stable.

Compare the Phases

The next step in the analytic procedure is to compare the phases using inferential statistics. For the purposes of action research, Cohen's effect size formula is a good measure to help you understand the magnitude of the difference between each phase. The effect size calculation is a little cumbersome in spreadsheet software, so let's break down the necessary steps.

The effect size formula uses the mean, standard deviation, and number of observations to calculate the difference between two distributions. To begin, we need to make a few adjustments to the table we already have started.

Sample Spreadsheet Table for Effect Size

	A	B	C	D
1		Mean	Standard_Deviation	Count
2	A1	7.6		
3	B1	2.7		
4	A2	5.6		

Next, add the standard deviation for each phase using the **STDEV.P** function. The syntax for this function is below. Having completed that step, add the total number of observations to your final column.

Syntax for the Standard Deviation, Population Function

=STDEV.P(range)
range   the selection of cells, usually a column, that contains the data that you want to summarize

Sample Spreadsheet Table for Effect Size, Complete

	A	B	C	D
1		Mean	Standard_Deviation	Count
2	A1	7.6	1.0	7
3	B1	2.7	0.9	7
4	A2	5.6	1.0	7

We want to know the magnitude of the difference between both the A1 and B1 phases and the B1 and A2 phases, so you will perform the effect size calculation twice.

You begin the effect size calculation by calculating the pooled standard deviation. The formula for pooled standard deviation is below. It looks a little tricky, so let's break it down. We are going to add together the product of the adjusted count of range one and the squared standard deviation of range one with the product of the adjusted count of range two and the squared standard deviation of range two. You will then divide that by the adjusted count of all scores. Finally, calculate the square root of that number, and you have the pooled standard deviation. Still confused? That's okay—just follow the formula below. That's why it's there. You can check yourself by using the numbers in the sample table above; the pooled standard deviation of this data is 0.97 for both the A1+B1 phases and the B1+A2 phases.

Syntax for the Pooled Standard Deviation Formula

$$=SQRT(((n1-1)*SD1\char94 2+(n2-1)*SD2\char94 2)/(n1+n2-2))$$

n_1	the count of range 1
SD_1	the standard deviation of range 1
n_2	the count of range 2
SD_2	the standard deviation of range 2

Finally, to calculate the effect size, you simply subtract the average of range one from the average of range two, then divide by your newly calculated pooled standard deviation. If you're following along with the data presented in this section, the effect size between phase A1 and B1 is 5.0 and between B1 and A2 is -2.9.

Syntax for the Effect Size Formula

$$=(M1-M2)/SDp$$

M_1	the mean (or average) of range 1
M_2	the mean (or average) of range 2
SDp	the pooled standard deviation

So what does this all mean? Effect sizes are pretty easy to interpret. Basically, the higher the effect size, the stronger the effect is determined to be. So with an effect size of 5.0, we can see that the intervention had a significant impact on our desired outcome, and since our second effect size is negative, we can see that taking the intervention away negatively impacted our desired outcome. The figures presented here have been exaggerated to make it easier to see; don't be surprised if your effect sizes are much smaller in reality.

Visualize the Phases

The final phase in the analysis of single-case data is the visualization phase. The unique style of visualization used in single-case analysis makes this study design a very reader-friendly research model. Single-case designs are visualized using line plots. Remember that a line plot is used to show changes over time; since we are looking at changes between phases, a line plot is a great way to go.

Line plot visualizations are easy to create in most spreadsheet software packages. Each package is different, so I have provided tutorial videos for some of the most common packages on the website that accompanies this book: https://www.matthewbcourtney.com/actionresearch. While the steps may vary, in general, you will highlight your selected data and then choose the line plot visualization from the visualization generator built into your spreadsheet software.

To make your plots even easier to see, it is common for practitioner researchers to include vertical lines that divide the plot into phases aligning to the timeline of your experiment. An example of this type of plot is below.

Sample Single-Case Design Visualization

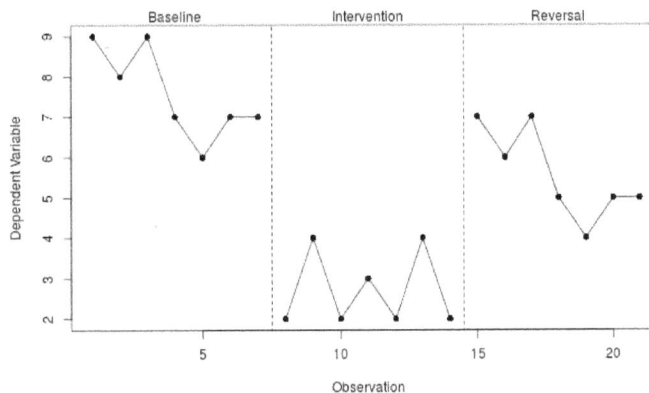

You can see that this plot makes it very easy for the reader to understand how your subject performed across each observation and throughout the three phases.

Online Tools

While I think it is beneficial to learn to manually perform each of the analytic steps presented here, I have also provided you with an online tool that can make this data analysis even easier. You can access the tool at https://www.matthewbcourtney.com/actionresearch. The Intervention Analysis Tool will take information you upload as a .CSV file and will automatically calculate the averages and effect sizes for each phase. It will also present three versions of the visualization for you to choose from.

To increase your success with using the tool, convert your data into a spreadsheet like the one below. Be sure to save it as a .CSV file before uploading. If you have any trouble, you can find additional support by accessing the tutorial video that goes along with the tool.

Sample Spreadsheet for Uploading to the Intervention Analysis Tool

	A	B
1	Phase	Score
2	A1	8
3	A1	7
4	A1	9
7	B1	3
8	B1	2
9	B1	1
10	C1	5
12	C1	3
13	C1	4
14	etc.…	etc.…

CHOOSE YOUR PATH

Now that you have completed your data analysis, turn to page 101 to learn how to make an evidence-informed decision.

Qualitative Coding

Coding is the process of sorting qualitative data into generalizable categories so that a large body of text can be more easily understood. You will want to deploy a qualitative coding protocol if the data that you collected through your study consists of a large body of text, such as open-ended survey questions, interview responses, or document reviews.

When you perform a coding protocol, it is very important that you document your process in a clear and transparent way. You should be able to explain your coding protocol in sufficient detail so that another researcher could take your raw data, deploy your protocol, and get a very similar result. It is important to note that the results of a qualitative coding protocol will never be exactly the same when performed by two different researchers–or even by the same researcher years apart. Qualitative coding requires a modicum of professional judgment.

To help ease the burden of communicating about qualitative coding protocols, there are established methodologies that you can follow and refer to. Below are five qualitative coding protocols that are most relevant to the action research framework:

- Attribute Coding: Attribute coding requires the researcher to assign codes to textual data that are aligned to a characteristic of the study participant. For example, a researcher may choose to deploy attribute coding when examining feedback on upcoming dress code changes if they want to know how female students feel about the new dress code compared to male students. In this case, the researcher would code each comment by the attribute "female" or "male."

- Concept Coding: Concept coding allows the researcher to group and summarize participant comments by macro level descriptors. These are usually short words or phrases that capture the essence or key theme of a group of comments. Concept coding may be useful in a situation where the researcher is trying to understand the feedback collected during a community forum related to a school's budget surplus.

The researcher may see common themes start to emerge organically from the solicited comments. For example, a group of participants may have expressed a desire for the school to use a budget surplus to renovate the playground and add new exercise equipment, while another group of participants may have advocated for the funds to be used for more nutritious food in the cafeteria. In this instance, the terms "playground equipment" and "nutritious food" may be effect terms to use during a conceptual coding protocol.

- Emotional Coding: Emotional coding is a technique in which the researcher sorts comments by the underlying emotions being expressed by the participants. This could be as simple as sorting comments into two categories: those in favor of a decision and those opposed to it, for example. A researcher may also find that there are more nuanced emotions buried within the comments. A series of comments opposed to a decision may also include emotions such as fear, anger, disappointment, or sadness.

- En Vivo Coding: En vivo coding is a technique that generates codes from the participants' own words or phrases. The researcher scans through each comment in the text and works to identify commonly used phrases. This can be especially useful in open-ended survey data where participants may have a more narrow scope of comments.

- Descriptive Coding: Descriptive coding is the most straightforward of all coding protocols. When deploying descriptive coding techniques, the researcher summarizes comments using descriptive adjectives of nouns. As they work through the body of comments, some descriptors may begin to align to one another. Descriptive coding requires a little more professional judgment than the other coding methods described herein.

Regardless of which coding method you choose, the process is pretty straightforward. Start by gathering all your comments and tidying them up so they are easy to work with. While you can work directly in a body of text or in word processing software, I recommend using spreadsheet software for this task. Place each comment in its own row in the first column. Next, simply read each comment and assign it a code. If you are using a spreadsheet to document your codes, you should place those in the second column. Once you have assigned codes to all the comments, you can begin to summarize them.

Let's look at an example. The image on the next page presents a series of comments shared during a public forum related to expanding a school's library. You can see that they are neatly aligned in a spreadsheet. In the second column, I have used descriptive coding to assign a code to each comment. Once the coding process is complete, we can see that there are still a lot of questions and concerns related to the school's planned library expansion. Three commenters are flatly opposed to the project, and no commenters gave clear indication that they are in favor of the expansion. The top concerns among those in attendance at the forum is the budgetary impact of the decision as well as ensuring that the library includes a wide variety of materials. There is also interest in promoting a clean and safe environment for students before and after school and increasing student access to technology.

Qualitative Coding Model Spreadsheet

	A	B
1	**Comment**	**Code**
2	The library is big enough.	Opposed
3	How are we going to pay for this expansion?	Budget
4	Students need access to books on a variety of concepts.	Variety
5	Will the expansion include only fiction books, or will non-fiction and reference books be included?	Variety
6	Will any programs be cut in order to fund the expansion?	Budget
7	What types of new technology will be added to the library?	Technology
8	I think the library needs to have a computer lab with a 3D printer.	Technology
9	My child prefers to read magazines and comic books.	Variety
10	I think we should take up donations to help off-set the cost of the expansion.	Budget
11	If you expand the library, I am moving to another community. We need other things.	Opposed
12	Will there be comfortable places for students to sit and read after school?	Environment
13	Who will staff the library after school? Can we afford that?	Budget
14	Will kids be able to check out iPads?	Technology
15	I don't think kids should be spending time in the library outside of the school day. They need to be outside!	Opposed
16	Will there be newspaper subscriptions?	Variety
17	I am concerned that couches may be difficult to keep clean.	Environment

You can see that this brief coding demonstration yielded detailed summary information that can be clearly reported on and allow the practitioner researcher to deeply discuss the concerns of the community in a detailed and thoughtful way.

As you conduct your coding protocol, you should also consider how you will best share the insights you cultivated from the body of text. In our library example, you could produce a table that summarizes the outcome of the coding protocol like the one below.

Model Data Table

Code	Count	Percent of Total
Opposed	3	18.7%
Budget	4	25.0%
Variety	4	25.0%
Technology	3	18.7%
Environment	2	12.5%

It could also be appropriate to pull illustrative quotes out of your text sample to demonstrate the underlying message behind each code. For example, it is helpful to know that twelve and a half percent of the comments were related to environment, but by adding the illustrative quote "Will there be comfortable places for students to sit and read after school?" we can provide more detail to help our audience understand the meaning behind the codes that we selected.

CHOOSE YOUR PATH

Now that you have completed your data analysis, turn to page 101 to learn how to make an evidence-informed decision.

Making Evidence-Informed Decisions

Now that you have completed your action research project, it is time to use your findings to inform the decisions you are making in your classroom. It is wonderful to be able to report sound research findings related to your problem of practice, but if you cannot clearly articulate why your findings are important and what they mean for the profession at large, then the results are not likely to lead to any meaningful change. In this section, we will explore how to take your findings and give them relevance that can lead to meaningful decisions, and we will discuss ways that you can use your findings to tell an impactful story.

Decision-making is the most challenging part of leadership, but with the help of your completed action research project, you are well positioned to make an evidence-informed decision that will help you, your students, and your colleagues. Remember that action research is a continuous improvement construct. It is a method designed to facilitate lasting, systemic improvements in your classroom, school, or system. Your project has consequence–it was intentionally designed that way–but it is up to you to apply your new learnings and figure out how to transform those learnings into actions. Let's think through the phases of evidence-informed decision-making.

Go Back to the Beginning

It has been a long time since you first started thinking about your original problem of practice. It is likely that the action research experience has helped you to see your original problem of practice in a new light. Your understanding has likely shifted, and the way you would explain your problem of practice today is probably different than how you would have described it at the beginning.

Before you can use your action research findings to inform your decision-making processes, you need to go back to the beginning of your project and think about the circumstances that led you here. Start with the problem itself. Reflect on the conditions that surrounded your problem several weeks ago. What specific challenges were you facing? What historical challenges were underpinning your problem? What solutions had you tried in the past?

Think about the emotions that coincided with your problem of practice. Did you feel frustrated? Scared? Confused? Disoriented? Allow these emotions to remind you why you took on this problem in the first place. By grounding yourself in that past state, you will be better prepared to make and communicate a decision that is grounded in your research findings.

Reflect on Your Data Analysis

Now that you have reminded yourself of the conditions surrounding your problem of practice, it is time to take a fresh look at your data analysis. Your data shows you a reflection of the efforts you have taken to solve the problem of practice. Through your data analysis, you will gain a deeper understanding of your proposed solution—an understanding that will inform your decision-making.

If you performed a study that included a qualitative coding protocol, start by looking at the various codes that you have assigned to your texts. What new themes have emerged for you through this process? It is likely that the coding process has validated some of your pre-existing notions about your problem of practice. It is equally likely that some themes may have challenged your opinions. It is also helpful to look beyond the themes and revisit the individual comments you coded. Choose a theme that challenged your thinking and reevaluate the comments with an open mind.

If you pursued a quantitative study, take time to consider the implications of the statistical analysis that you performed. Start by reviewing the descriptive statistics that you calculated. Remind yourself about each distribution of scores and what they represent. Remember: When we turn kids into numbers, we have to turn the numbers back into kids before we make a decision. Make an effort to see your students in those distributions and breathe life into the numbers. Data analysis is unemotional—decision-making is not.

One you have reviewed the descriptive statistics, consider the inferential statistics that you calculated. Were the results of your correlational analysis strong or weak, positive or negative? Were the results of your t-test statistically significant? Was the effect size large or small; is there practical significance to your results? Remember that your statistical outputs reflect only the intervention that you tested. Did your intervention work as you intended?

Use Literature to Provide Context

Once you have taken time to analyze and understand your data analysis, go back to the literature you reviewed at the onset of the study and allow it to provide additional context. If you performed a thorough and meaningful literature review, you should have identified trends and gaps in the literature that informed your study. Revisit those trends and gaps and consider how your findings fit in with the literature.

Allow the literature to help inform the story of your data. By placing your data in context with the existing literature, you will have a better understanding of the meaning of your project. It is likely that one of three things happened.

1. <u>Themes from the literature resonate with your study.</u> You may find that the themes you originally identified in your literature review align with your study outcomes. This is an indication that your thinking about the problem of practice is aligned with mainstream thinking on the issue. This may suggest that more solutions to your problem can be found through a deeper literature review.

2. <u>Your study fills a gap in the literature.</u> You may determine that your work has created new information about your problem of practice. If this is the case, your next task is to continue to innovate around your problem of practice until you find a solution that works for you. Think about the other systems and processes you may want to change as you continue to explore your problem of practice.

3. <u>Your study is not reflected in any part of the literature.</u> While uncommon, you may find that your study results simply do not resonate with the literature you reviewed. Perhaps the literature showed resounding, universal success of an intervention that didn't work for you. Or maybe an intervention that wasn't supposed to work actually did. In this instance, you should return to your study design and consider if factors in your study differed from other published studies in a way that may have changed the results. You should also consider whether your original literature review was thorough; maybe you missed something important. By understanding how and why your results differ, you will have a better foundation upon which to make your decision.

In the end, you want to be able to make a decision that is in alignment with both your research results and the full body of research on your problem of practice. This makes your decision stronger, better informed, and more defensible.

Consider Your Local Context

Along with a review of the literature, you want to consider the local context of your study before making a decision. True evidence-informed decisions blend local demands and capacities with the results of research to drive lasting and sustainable change.

Throughout your action research project, you likely encountered local issues that influenced your understanding of your problem of practice. Issues such as a lack of teacher time, state and federal programmatic constraints, or financial limitations can all impact the success of an intervention. Spend some time reflecting on how your project was impacted by factors outside of your control. Did a district leader move kids from your control group to the intervention group without your consent? Did the teacher *really* implement 40 extra minutes of reading instruction as you asked? Did the interviewees feel comfortable and confident to give their truthful answers? All of these environmental factors may impact your decision-making process.

It is also important for you to consider whether the results of your action research project can be replicated and sustained. A positive solution to a problem is only meaningful if other teachers can actually do it. For example, if your project was supported by one-time grant funds or you were given an extra planning period to monitor your project, you should consider whether it is something that can be repeated in the future without those added supports. It may be that replication is impossible or that some creative tweaking to your project may make it more sustainable.

Seek Input from Your Team

Teaching is a team sport; you don't have to make instructional decisions on your own. In fact, you really shouldn't! As you work to determine the potential implications of your research findings, consider pulling together a small team to help you reflect. Your professional learning community, or PLC, can be a great team to help you think through the implications of your work.

When seeking input on your research from your teammates, it is important to give them enough background information about your project so that they can understand what you did but to do so in a conversational way so that they feel open to provide the feedback you seek. Frame your conversation openly and honestly and encourage your peers to push back on your findings and dig deep through their feedback.

Decide, Implement, and Design a Monitoring Protocol

The final step in the decision-making process is to decide. As a leader and practitioner researcher, you must make the leap from your research project toward actual long-term implementation. Having considered your data, the literature, the local context, and feedback from trusted peers, you should have enough information to confidently make a decision about your next steps.

Regardless of your decision, it should come with an implementation and monitoring plan. Your action research project is only the beginning. To truly make a lasting change, you must implement it and monitor it over time. One of the best tools for monitoring a long-term change is the Plan-Do-Study-Act protocol, or PDSA. The PDSA is a cyclical tool in which you plan implementation steps, implement your change while collecting data, study the impact of the change, and make a new decision to improve or reinforce the change. This is a great way to hold yourselves and others accountable for making sure improvements stick. For more information about implementing a PDSA protocol, check out the online resources at https://www.matthewbcourtney.com/actionresearch.

CHOOSE YOUR PATH

The final step in your action research project is to share your results with your colleagues. Turn to page 107 for some tips on how to effectively communicate your results.

Communicating the Results of Research

Congratulations! You have done amazing work. You have identified a persistent problem of practice, designed and tested a solution, and made a decision that will change teaching and learning in your school or system. Now it's time to let the world know! Communicating the results of research is an important part of the process. By openly and transparently sharing your work with the world, you will elevate the entire teaching profession.

Key Elements to Communicate

When it comes to sharing the results of your action research project, there are a few standardized elements that other members of the research community will expect to see. Regardless of how you choose to present your findings, each of these elements should show up somewhere along the way.

1. Abstract: Your communication should begin with a brief abstract that summarizes your project from start to finish. Good abstracts are usually between two hundred and three hundred words and include a statement of purpose, one or two key literature review elements, a sentence about methodology, and a brief statement of key findings.

2. Introduction: Begin your communication by providing a brief, one- to two-paragraph introduction. This introduction should provide background on the current events or environmental changes that inspired your action research project.

3. Literature Review: In the literature review section of your communication, you will present the theoretical model you crafted earlier in this process. Use subheadings to keep your communication tidy and organized.

4. Methodology: The methodology section is where you share the steps you took to complete your action research project. You should discuss elements of your study design, information about your study participants, and a description of the analytic procedures you deployed to make sense of the data you collected. You may also need to include a discussion of the intervention you deployed.

5. Findings: This is the most important part of your research communications. This is where you will show your readers the actual results of your analysis.

6. Discussion: Following your findings, your communication should include a detailed discussion about your study overall. This is your chance to tell your audience why your results matter and how they might influence future decision-makers.

7. Conclusion: Wrap up your communication with a brief, usually one-paragraph, restatement of the key elements of your paper. This is your chance to highlight the most important things that you want your reader to remember.

8. References List: Regardless of your communication style, you should always include a comprehensive references list at the end. Your audience needs to know where to look for other information about your project and its themes.

Sharing a Compelling Research Story

Your research project is a wonderful and powerful thing, but it will not have meaning outside of your own context if you cannot tell a compelling story about your work. Storytelling is as important a part of effective research as it is effective teaching. Stories grab the reader's attention and speak to their imagination. They make it easier for the reader to connect to your work and to see themselves implementing your solutions in their classrooms.

In formal research, the storytelling component comes in the "Discussion" section of a research paper or presentation and is presented after the literature review, methodology, and results have already been discussed. This is the researcher's chance to provide nuance and suggest potential application strategies for their findings. Effective discussions are not mere re-statements of the results; rather, they seek to paint a picture in the mind of the reader.

One key element of effective research storytelling is a reflection on the potential application of the research findings. Effective authors weave elements from their literature review and examples from their study findings together to explain to the reader how their study findings can change teaching practice. It is important that this section be compelling without being hyperbolic. As the author, you should work to maintain an accurate review of your research results while presenting an honest narrative of its potential application.

Another way to effectively tell your research story is to explore how your study is situated within the literature that you have already discussed. Ideally, your literature review revealed gaps in understanding that your project is poised to fill. Explain to the reader how your study adds to the literature and fills in these important gaps.

Finally, an effective story section acknowledges the weaknesses in the current study and proposes future research project ideas that may help to overcome those weaknesses. No research project is ever perfect. As a practitioner researcher, you must be able to identify the quality gaps in your research and acknowledge those. These are called "limitations." Common limitations in the action research setting include small sample sizes, samples with limited diversity or world view, short timeframes, and less rigorous data collection methods or study designs.

When presenting the limitations to your current study, reflect on how those limitations may be overcome by yourself or a future researcher through revised study procedures. By proposing new studies that strengthen your own, you are showing your expertise and situational awareness. You may also help another researcher add to the literature on your problem of practice. You should also reflect on any new questions that your research has posed. Effective research always answers the question at hand while simultaneously revealing new questions to be explored. These new questions add richness and depth to the research story you are trying to tell and compel the reader to continue to think about your project once they have finished your story.

In formal presentations, you should wrap up with a succinct conclusion. Your conclusion should recapitulate your study by clearly re-stating the problem of practice and research question, providing a one-sentence summary of your methodology, reviewing one or two key findings, and restating the key implementation takeaway from your work.

Let's take a deeper dive into the three most common modalities for sharing your research story with the world: research papers, research presentations, and research posters.

The Research Paper

As professionals, we have an obligation to share our work with the field to inform and shape modern best practices. One of the most powerful and lasting ways to communicate the results of your action research project is through writing and publication. Once a piece of research is published in a peer-reviewed journal, it lives on forever.

Publishing a paper in an academic journal is a worthy pursuit yet not for the faint of heart. The process can be challenging, time-consuming, and is often ego-bruising. However, if you are prepared with the proper training and expectations, your work can appear in one of the nation's leading journals!

The first thing you need is an original academic study. No journal will publish work that has already been published or is being considered for publication elsewhere. Journal articles are not like blog posts or presentations at educational conferences–they can only be shared once. This is part of what makes academic publishing so time-consuming. You can only submit one piece of work to one journal at a time. You stop to consider your publication options when your journal article is *almost* ready (more on why later).

Once your manuscript is *almost* ready to go, the next step is to select a journal with which you will pursue publication. A simple Internet search will reveal the journals most likely to publish your paper. Simply take your theme and add the word *journal* to the end and see what pops up. For example, if your action research project is about library sciences, consider an Internet search for "journal of library sciences." This search process will yield many possible journals that you could consider.

One of the key elements to getting your manuscript published is submitting it to the right journal. To do this, you must read about the journal's "scope." The scope is the span of work that the journal specializes in–or is specializing in right now. It is important to note that the scope of a journal may not always align with its title, and scopes can change over time as journals seek to remain relevant in the current publishing environment. If your paper is not aligned with the scope of the journal, do not submit. An unaligned scope is the number one reason for a desk rejection–meaning the editor says no without even reading your paper. Here are a couple of other things you may want to consider when choosing a journal:

- Does the journal publish papers that you want to read? If not, you may not get your research in the hands of the right audience.

- Is the journal open sourced or subscription based? Generally, open-sourced articles are viewed more frequently than subscription-based journals, but they sometimes charge publication fees to offset the lost revenue that a subscription would bring. Weigh these options carefully.

- Does the editorial board include respected members of your research community? If you don't recognize any of the names on the editorial board, do a quick search to see what kind of work they have done in the past. If you don't like the members on the board, you probably won't like the journal.

- Does the journal deploy a peer review process? Most academic journals do, but there are multiple peer review models that coincide with various levels of rigor and time. Make sure you fully understand the peer review process of the journal before you submit to it.

- Does the journal have a good impact factor? The impact factor is a statistical measure that attempts to show how important a journal is. In education, impact factors are not always reported, and this step really only matters if you are trying to be a tenured professor at a Carnegie Research University. The higher the impact factor, the more influential a journal is. You must decide how much that matters to you.

Having chosen the journal that you want to submit to, it is time to finalize your manuscript. Every journal will include detailed instructions for the author to prepare the manuscript for submission. This is why it is important to select a journal when your manuscript is *almost* ready. It will save you time on the back end. Ultimately, it doesn't matter what the style guide handbooks say or how you were taught to write in college. What matters is that you meet the rules of the journal you submit to. If the journal says to include a 300-word abstract, include a 300-word abstract—not a 305-word abstract or a 293-word abstract. If the journal tells you to submit as a PDF, submit as a PDF. If the journal tells you to include the name of each author of a paper in your in-text citation, your paper should follow suit. Follow their rules exactly if you want to increase your chances of being published.

When your manuscript is complete, follow the submission processes on the journal's website. Some journals ask you to simply email your manuscript to the editor. Others want you to create accounts and fill out online forms. Follow their directions, click Submit, and wait.

Waiting is a key element of the publication process. Articles can go from manuscript to publication in as little as a month or sometimes longer than a year, and it is totally out of your hands at this point. Put the paper out of your mind and wait for a decision.

Speaking of decisions, there are generally five editorial decisions for academic papers. They are as follows:

1. Desk rejection: A desk rejection means that the editor doesn't think that your paper is a good fit for their journal and therefore will not send it to peer review. Desk rejections are quick, and there is no coming back from one. Simply pick a new journal and try again.

2. Rejection: A rejection means that the peer reviewers have reviewed your paper and believe that it is not of sufficient quality for publication in the specific journal. Usually, a rejection comes with a detailed explanation (about a page) that tells you why the article was rejected for publication. The rejection may or may not invite you to resubmit your paper after you make significant changes. If you get a rejection, carefully re-edit your paper based on the feedback and submit to a new journal.

3. Revise and Resubmit: A revise and resubmit means that the peer reviewers and editors felt that your paper was of sufficient merit to be published but that it needs substantial edits before they can do so. The decision letter will tell you what changes the reviewers

want to see. Generally, a revise and resubmit comes with a deadline (2-4 weeks) and a requirement that you provide a letter to the editor outlining the changes made to your paper. After you resubmit, the paper is reviewed again, usually by the same peer reviewers as before.

4. Accept with Revisions: A decision of accept with revisions means that the peer reviewers and editors feel that your paper is of sufficient quality to be published but may need minor revisions before publication. For example, if you are publishing in an international journal, they may ask you to make changes to spelling conventions or swap out certain country-specific vocabulary for a more generic international alternative. Simply make these changes and resubmit to the editor. An accept with revisions is rarely re-considered by the peer review team.

5. Accept: A decision of accept is the rarest of gems. This means that everyone involved believes that your paper is ready for immediate publication. Celebrate! You are done, and your paper will be appearing in the journal soon!

This process can feel like a deeply personal process, and even the most experienced researchers go through a wide range of emotions when working through the academic publication process. Feel your feelings, then put them aside. Do not let negative emotions derail you from your goal of sharing your important work with the world. It is not uncommon for researchers to submit a single paper to multiple journals before finally getting an acceptance. That is simply part of the process.

If you need more help thinking through how a research paper should be presented to your audience, check out the annotated research paper mockup in *Appendix C: Papers, Posters, and Presentations*.

The Research Presentation

A research conference is very different than the professional learning conferences experienced by most educators. In a research conference, program organizers review submitted research proposals, accept the proposals that meet their quality standards, and group them into strands for delivery.

Generally, a one-hour session will include presentations from four to five different researchers whose work is on a similar topic. These presentations are extremely limited on time. They do not include many of the hallmarks of education conferences, such as ice breakers, activities, or audience participation beyond clarifying questions. They are direct, succinct, and hurried.

To get on the agenda at a research conference, you will typically be asked to prepare and submit a proposal during a brief window of time–usually around eight to ten months before the conference is scheduled. The key to success here is to follow the directions! Different conferences ask for different things. Most of them will ask you to describe your problem, methodology, key findings, and implications in less than 1000 words.

If you happen to have an action research project selected for presentation during a research conference, your brief presentation requires careful planning. During your presentation, you will want to discuss all the sections you would have included had you chosen to present your research in a written format. You should start with a brief introduction about yourself. Be sure to tell who you are and why you are the right person to work on this topic. Next, you will want to briefly mention the key points from the literature. Include a couple of citations for the most important supporting pieces of literature that informed your work. This is followed by a brief discussion about your methods. Don't belabor the point here. Tell the audience what you did and why you did it, then move on. Finally, you want to talk about your results and why your results matter.

Generally, it is best if you discuss the relevance of each finding along the way, rather than presenting all your findings and circling back to relevance at the end. If you have time, it is also good to talk about the next steps and future research potential of your topic area. Be sure you include a full references list on the last slide and your contact information.

After your presentation, you should be prepared to take questions from the audience. Different conferences have different methods for facilitating this process. Generally, audience members will be allowed to ask clarifying questions and offer suggestions for future study. This is an opportunity for you to further discuss the importance of your work and solicit feedback that will make your work stronger in the future.

As a side note, while you are there to highlight the important research work you have conducted, the value of well-constructed slides cannot be underrepresented. You could present Nobel Prize-worthy research, but if you do it in such a way that the audience cannot follow along, it will not be well received. Here are five things to consider when designing slides:

1. Use a branded logo template. If your organization has a standardized branded template, you should use that to present your work. Odds are good that the branded template was designed by someone with an eye for presentations.

2. Use high contrasting colors. Black and white is best. Remember, you will likely be using someone else's technology, and you never know how the images on your screen will translate to the images on their screen.

3. Keep the font big and text density low. If you need two slides to present your findings effectively, use two slides. If the audience is busy reading your screen, they are not listening to you.

4. Use charts over tables. While tables are great at showing the nuances of your data in a written format, they are not great for viewing from the audience. Visual charts are always a better option when available.

5. Don't fill the slide with unnecessary images. White space is okay—in fact, it is preferred. Do not add photos of your students, classrooms, or student work samples unless they are explicitly related to the findings in your study.

For more information on presenting a beautiful and effective research presentation, check out the slide mockups found in *Appendix C: Papers, Posters, and Presentations.*

The Research Poster

Most research conferences receive more proposals than they can feasibly support in their sessions. To create space, many conferences offer the opportunity to participate in poster sessions. During a poster session, researchers prepare posters about their research and present their work as other conference attendees peruse the gallery. It is kind of like a high school science fair on steroids.

Poster sessions are great opportunities to share your work in a more casual way. They are good for new researchers who are still finding their footing because they provide a safer atmosphere to discuss research one on one with interested parties. They are also great for presenting work that is in early stages, such as preliminary results from a multi-year analysis.

Generally, your poster should include all the same sections that you would include in journal articles or presentation slides, but the overall design of your poster and brevity of your language become even more important. I have included some mockups of poster designs in *Appendix C: Papers, Posters, and Presentations.* Here are a few tips to help you create beautiful academic posters.

• Always check your acceptance notification for acceptable poster dimensions. Most conferences will provide you with an easel and back-board to place your poster, but you don't want to bring a poster that will not fit on the supplied display surface.

- Make sure you use calm and coordinated colors. Your poster should be easily readable from a distance of four feet, which means that your poster should have high color contrast.

- Make your results easily readable and place them in a prime location–usually the middle. When a fellow researcher approaches your work, they will likely read your title first and then move directly to your results.

- Ensure that your poster maintains a clear flow of communication. You don't want your readers searching for what they should read next.

- Distill your work down to neat bullet points when possible. Nobody is going to stand and read your poster for twenty minutes.

- Include your contact information, headshot, and organization logo. This makes it easy for other researchers to find you after the fact.

- Be prepared to talk and engage people about your research. Poster sessions are all about one-on-one interaction. While fewer people will be exposed to your work, those who are will have a richer, deeper experience if you are prepared to talk about the finer points.

CHOOSE YOUR PATH

Congratulations! You have reached the end of your adventure. After you share your results with your colleagues, you are ready to reap the rewards of your hard work. Sit back and watch your improvements take shape.

Afterword

Well, you made it! Congratulations and thank you for sticking with me to the very end. I hope that this book has been a source of inspiration and education for you as you begin to think more deeply about how you may use action research techniques to improve teaching and learning conditions in your school or system.

Remember that action research is merely a framework for decision-making, and it is ultimately what you make of it. Consider ways to embed action research protocols into your usual planning and improvement cycles. I recommend that you make a public commitment to perform at least one action research cycle per year. This will ensure that you truly become a practitioner of <u>continuous</u> improvement.

I am a big believer in continuous school improvement. I believe it is how we make good schools great and great schools even better. By reflecting on your own action research work and challenging yourself to resolve persistent problems of practice, you will be well on your way to a brighter future. I want to help you get there! If the material presented in this book has been meaningful to you, please consider visiting my website (<u>https://www.matthewbcourtney.com/</u>) to check out the other resources that I offer.

A good place to start is The Repository (<u>https://www.matthewbcourtney.com/repository</u>). The Repository houses all of my online continuous improvement and data analysis tools. You will find the auto-analysis tools discussed throughout this book, tutorial videos to help you learn new data analysis and research skills, free e-books and resources to help supplement your library, and premium online course modules to help you dig deeper into important topics related to continuous improvement.

I also hope that you will consider subscribing to my weekly blog, #BeyondTheMean (<u>https://www.matthewbcourtney.com/blog</u>). Through #BeyondTheMean, I present case studies, tutorials, and thought articles about the various ways that data analysis and research can be used to drive continuous school improvement in a meaningful way. I am all about stripping out the complex theory and presenting the content in a way that is accessible and approachable. I want you to be successful, and my blog posts are designed to give you weekly food for thought to help keep you focused.

Finally, I would love to visit your institution and talk with your colleagues about continuous improvement. I offer trainings and workshops on a wide variety of continuous improvement topics, including action research processes. I have spoken to thousands of teachers across the nation and presented at many national conferences. I want to help your team build capacity for meaningful data and research use to drive continuous improvement. You can reach out by completing the training request form on my website (https://www.matthewbcourtney.com/training).

I wish you the best of luck and all the success in the world as you continue your adventure into the world of continuous improvement. I hope that you will consider me a friend and resource as you learn and grow. Be kind to yourself as you learn and try to embrace the productive disequilibrium you feel. Push through the discomfort and frustration that accompanies new learnings, and you will reap the rewards at the end. When in doubt, focus on your students and let them motivate you to achieve greatness.

Good luck on your journey, friend!

Appendix A: Citation Management

As you prepare your work for public consumption, you should consider how you will present citations to your reader. Regardless of whether you choose to present a research paper, poster, or presentation, proper citation of your sources is vital to your success as a practitioner researcher.

Using citations not only provide you with additional credibility, but also elevates the work of others and shows respect to the researchers who came before you. In education, it is most common to use the American Psychological Association (APA) format for citations; however, each journal, research conference, and college professor will have their own nuances for how you should prepare citations. If you are completing your work within a context that does not provide clear guidance on citation formatting, you should follow the basic rules below.

- In-Text Citations
    - Use in-text citations within the content of your written literature review or at the end of each bullet on a literature review presentation slide.
    - In-text citations go inside parentheses and before the period.
    - Use author last names only.
    - Citation models:
        - One author: (Author, Year).
        - Two authors: (Author & Author, Year).
        - Three or more authors: (Author, et. al., Year).
        - Multiple citations in one sentence: (Author, Year; Author, Year).

- References List
    - Your references list should start at the top of a fresh page in a research paper or on a fresh slide on a research presentation.
    - Your citation should include the author, year, and all relevant publication information to help your audience find those articles for later review.
    - References lists should be formatted using a one-inch hanging indent.
    - Reference Formatting Models
        - Academic Journal Article; Single Author
            - Author Last Name, Initial. Initial. (Year). This is my title: This is my subtitle. *The Academic Journal*, Volume(edition). DOI: xxxxxxxxxxxxxxxxxxxxxxxxxxxxxxxxxxxxxxxx
        - Academic Journal Article; Two Authors
            - Author Last Name, Initial. Initial., Author Last name, Initial. Initial. (Year). This is my title: This is my subtitle. *The Academic*

Journal, Volume(edition). DOI: xxxxxxxxxxxxxxxxxxxxxxxxxxxxxxxx

- Academic Journal Article; Three or More Authors
  - Author Last Name, Initial. Initial., Author Last Name, Initial. Initial., Author Last Name, Initial. Initial. (Year). This is my title: This is my subtitle. *The Academic Journal*, Volume(edition). DOI: xxxxxxxxxxxxxxxxxxxxxxxxxxxxxxxx
- Book, One Author
  - Author Last Name, Initial. Initial. (Year). *This is my book title*. Publisher.
- Book, Two Authors
  - Author Last Name, Initial. Initial., Author Last Name, Initial. Initial. (Year). *This is my book title*. Publisher.
- Book, Three or More Authors
  - Author Last Name, Initial. Initial., Author Last Name, Initial. Initial., Author Last Name, Initial. Initial. (Year). *This is my book title*. Publisher.
- Federal Statute
  - Title, Number U.S.C. § Section Number (Subsection Number).
- State Statute
  - Title, Number. State.
- Administrative Regulation
  - Title, Number, State.
- Government Document
  - Government Agency (Year). *This is my title*. Retrieved from: website
- Public Data Sets
  - Agency (Year). *Title of Data Set* [data set]. Retrieved from: website

Appendix B: Formatting Charts and Tables

Your final action research project likely includes a variety of tables and charts. Proper formatting ensures that your audience will be able to read and understand your tables and charts easily and accurately. While each journal, research conference, and college professor will have their own rules for formatting tables and charts, this appendix includes some general rules to consider.

Table Formatting

A properly formatted table goes a long way toward ensuring that your final product looks professional. Unless otherwise specified, here are some general rules to consider when preparing tables:

- Tables should be printed in the same font as the surrounding text.
- Tables can be either right aligned or center aligned within a body of text. Pick one alignment structure to use throughout your project.
- Tables should be titled and numbered on the line immediately preceding the chart.
- Table titles should be presented in sentence case.
- Tables should include only horizontal lines. They should include a top and bottom line as well as a line separating a heading from the data presented.
- Within a table, headings should be center aligned within a cell. Text in the first column should be right aligned within its cell, while data presented in the additional columns should be center aligned under their headings.
- Table footnotes should be placed directly beneath the bottom line and usually two sizes smaller than the surrounding font.

Formatting Charts

Like tables, a well-formatted chart can help your audience understand your data by presenting it in a visual format. As a rule, less is more when it comes to data visualization. Stick to standard chart formats that your audience is likely to understand. Here are a few things to consider:

- Charts should be printed in the same font as the surrounding text.

- Charts can be either right aligned or center aligned within a body of text. Pick one alignment structure to use throughout your project.
- Charts should be titled and numbered on the line immediately preceding the chart.
- Chart titles should be presented in sentence case.
- Chart footnotes should be placed directly beneath the bottom line and usually two sizes smaller than the surrounding font.
- Charts should be presented in black and white. When differentiation between data elements is necessary, consider using symbols or labels.
- Choose the correct chart design for the data being presented.
  - Choose a boxplot to represent a distribution of data.
  - Chose a line plot to represent changes over time.
  - Choose a scatter plot to represent the relationship between two variables.
  - Choose a bar plot to visually compare two variables.
  - Choose a histogram to represent statistical dispersion.

Formatting Models

Below are three models to demonstrate how charts and tables should be formatted within the context of your action research project. Remember that your chosen journal, research conference, or college professor may have different guidelines for you to follow.

Table Formatting Model

Figure 1: This is my sample table title.

	Variable	Variable	Variable	Variable
Variable	##	##	##	##
Variable	##	##	##	##
Variable	##	##	##	##

This is my footnote.

Boxplot Formatting Model

Figure 1: This is my sample chart title.

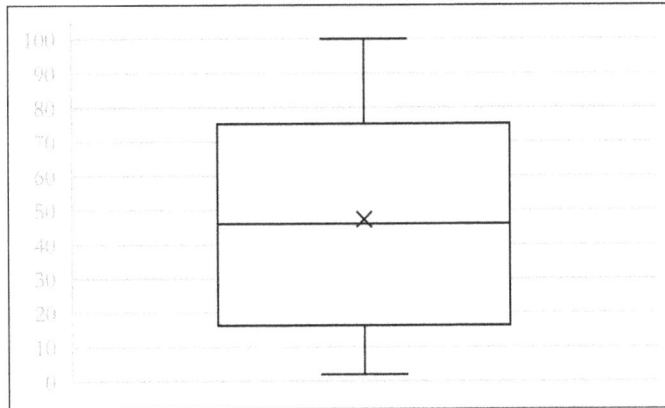

This is my footnote.

Scatterplot Formatting Model

Figure 1: This is my sample chart title.

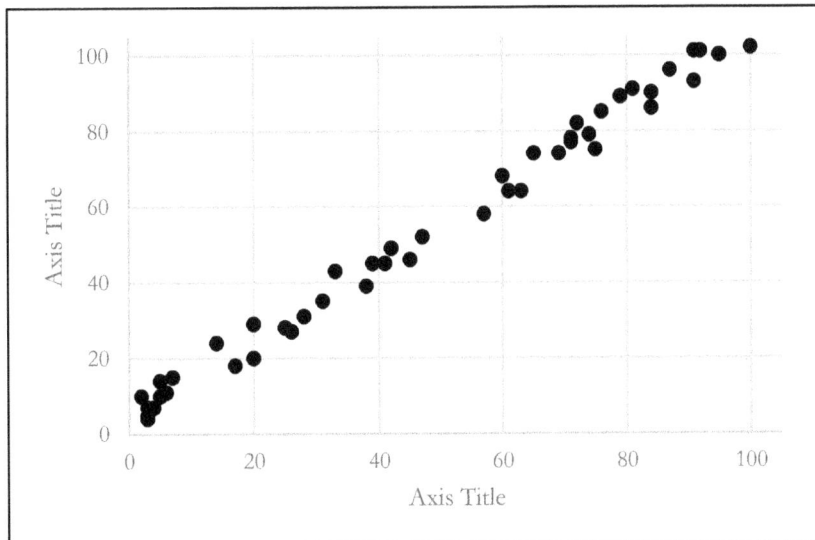

This is my footnote.

Appendix C:
Papers, Posters, and Presentations

While every institution, publication, and event will have its own expectations for how your research should be formatted, the examples here are provided as general guidelines to help you share the results of your action research projects more easily.

The Research Paper

Research papers usually require a cover page that includes the title of your project, your name, your institution, and the date.

Following the cover page, you should begin the second page with your abstract. The abstract should be roughly 150-250 words and should summarize your project in such a way as to allow the reader to determine if your project is relevant to them.

The text of the paper itself begins after the abstract, usually following an "Introduction" heading. The rest of your paper should flow following the order of the steps you have completed throughout this book. Unless otherwise instructed, format your paper using Times New Roman font with a 12-point size and double spaced.

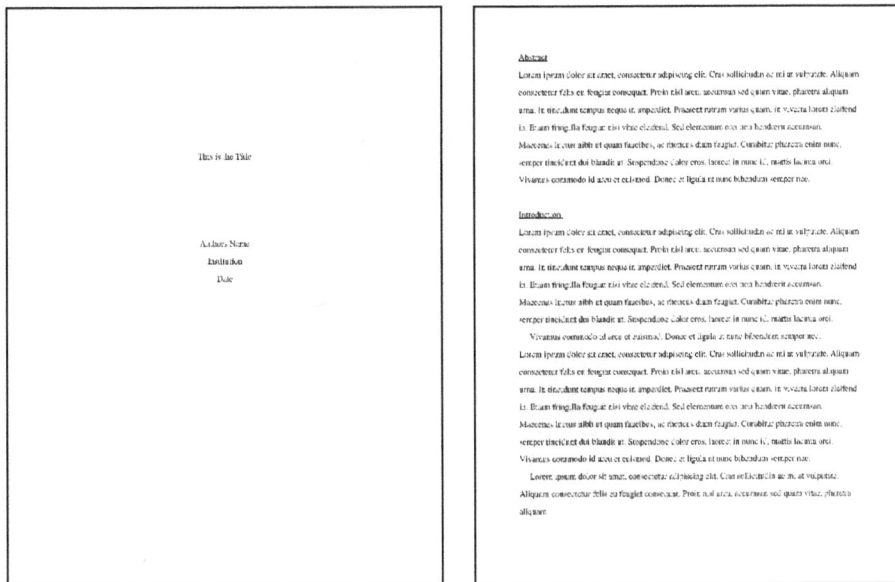

The Research Poster

Research posters should contain all the same information and headings as a research paper, but in a much more condensed format. Before preparing your research poster, you should check to see the required dimensions; usually posters are somewhere between three and four feet tall and four and five feet wide. Remember to keep your comments brief, include charts and visualizations, and be sure to list your contact information.

Remember that most people won't have time to read your poster in detail. It is a good idea to provide copies of your written paper or include a QR code that conference participants can scan to download more details about your project.

The Research Presentation

When preparing presentation slides, it is important to consider the viewers' perspective. Remember that presentation slides are not for you; they should not include all the details you want to reference during your presentation. Keep your slides neat and tidy and use contrasting colors so your audience can read what you included. In a research presentation, each heading should go on its own slide.

This is the title.
Practitioner Researcher's Name

Literature Review

- Important information from the literature (citation).
- Important information from the literature (citation).
- Important information from the literature (citation).

Methodology

- Important detail about how you conducted the study.
- Important detail about how you conducted the study.
- Important detail about how you conducted the study.
- Important detail about how you conducted the study.
- Important detail about how you conducted the study.

Findings

- Key finding
- Key finding
- Key finding
- Key finding

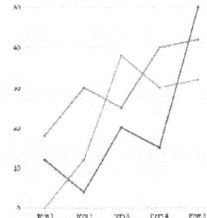

Discussion

- Important detail you want the audience to know.
- Important detail you want the audience to know.
- Important detail you want the audience to know.
- Important detail you want the audience to know.
- Important detail you want the audience to know.
- Important detail you want the audience to know.

References

- Last, F.M. (YYYY). This is the title of the reference. *This is the title of the journal (#)#.* Pg - Pg. DOI: XXXXXXXXXXXXXXXXXX
- Last, F.M. (YYYY). This is the title of the reference. This is the title of the journal (#)#. Pg - Pg. DOI: XXXXXXXXXXXXXXXXXX
- Last, F.M. (YYYY). This is the title of the reference. This is the title of the journal (#)#. Pg - Pg. DOI: XXXXXXXXXXXXXXXXXX
- Last, F.M. (YYYY). This is the title of the reference. This is the title of the journal (#)#. Pg - Pg. DOI: XXXXXXXXXXXXXXXXXX
- Last, F.M. (YYYY). This is the title of the reference. This is the title of the journal (#)#. Pg - Pg. DOI: XXXXXXXXXXXXXXXXXX
- Last, F.M. (YYYY). This is the title of the reference. This is the title of the journal (#)#. Pg - Pg. DOI: XXXXXXXXXXXXXXXXXX

Index

Notes

Notes

Notes

Notes

Notes

Notes

Notes

www.ingramcontent.com/pod-product-compliance
Lightning Source LLC
Chambersburg PA
CBHW080404270326
41927CB00015B/3343